Ethics of Compassion

For Lopa,
Living with Indian
Wisdom & American opportunity —
What an adventure!
Warm regards,
Richard Reilly
Dec 2008

STUDIES IN COMPARATIVE PHILOSOPHY AND RELIGION

Series Editor: Douglas Allen, University of Maine

This series explores important intersections within and between the disciplines of religious studies and philosophy. These original studies will emphasize, in particular, aspects of contemporary and classical Asian philosophy and its relationship to Western thought. We welcome a wide variety of manuscript submissions, especially works exhibiting highly focused research and theoretical innovation.

Varieties of Ethical Reflection: New Directions for Ethics in a Global Context, by Michael Barnhart

Mysticism and Morality: A New Look at Old Questions, by Richard H. Jones

Gandhi's Experiments with Truth: Essential Writings by and about Mahatma Gandhi, by Richard L. Johnson

To Broaden the Way: A Confucian–Jewish Dialogue, by Galia Patt-Shamir

Pyrrhonism: How the Ancient Greeks Reinvented Buddhism, by Adrian Kuzminski

Ethics of Compassion: Bridging Ethical Theory and Religious Moral Discourse, by Richard Reilly

Ethics of Compassion

Bridging Ethical Theory and Religious Moral Discourse

RICHARD REILLY

LEXINGTON BOOKS

A division of
ROWMAN & LITTLEFIELD PUBLISHERS, INC.
Lanham • Boulder • New York • Toronto • Plymouth, UK

LEXINGTON BOOKS

A division of Rowman & Littlefield Publishers, Inc.
A wholly owned subsidary of The Rowman & Littlefield Publishing Group, Inc.
4501 Forbes Boulevard, Suite 200
Lanham, MD 20706

Estover Road
Plymouth PL6 7PY
United Kingdom

Copyright © 2008 by Lexington Books

British Library Cataloguing in Publication Information Available

Library of Congress Cataloging-in-Publication Data

Reilly, Richard, 1944–
  Ethics of compassion : bridging ethical theory and religious moral discourse / Richard
Reilly.
      p. cm. — (Studies in comparative philosophy and religion)
  Includes bibliographical references and index.
  ISBN-13: 978-0-7391-2504-5 (cloth : alk. paper)
  ISBN-10: 0-7391-2504-4 (cloth : alk. paper)
  ISBN-13: 978-0-7391-3145-9 (electronic)
  ISBN-10: 0-7391-3145-1 (electronic)
  1. Compassion. 2. Golden rule. 3. Religion and ethics. I. Title.
  BJ1475.R45 2008
  177'.7—dc22   2008030419

Printed in the United States of America

For Brenda

Contents

Acknowledgments

I wish to express my appreciation to St. Bonaventure University for a sabbatic leave for calendar year 2002 which enabled me to research and draft Chapters I-V of this book. Since then I had the privilege to present my work piecemeal at departmental colloquia as well as at conferences sponsored by the Society of Asian and Comparative Philosophy (2004 and 2006), by the Society for Buddhist-Christian Studies (2005) and by the Society for Christian Philosophers (2006). I am indebted to my departmental colleagues and to conference participants for many thoughtful questions, comments and criticisms that led to improvements in my analyses and line of argumentation. I especially wish to thank Professor Donald Swearer for encouraging me to prepare an article for the *Journal of Buddhist-Christian Studies*, 23 (2006) that covers much of what appears here as Chapters I and III, to Professor Allen W. Wood for detailed comments that brought Kantian ethics into clearer focus for me, and to Professor Robert Kane, whose work and communications were vital to my completing, after many years of on-again, off-again attempts, the libertarian account of free will and responsibility appearing in Chapter VI.

I am deeply grateful to Professor Herbert Fingarette, who, for some forty years has inspired me as teacher, author and friend to attend to fundamental truths of humanity that underlie and give life to cultural forms and traditions. What understanding of compassion I have been able to attain is due to my dharma teacher, H.E. Shyalpa Rinpoche; and whatever I lack in practicing what I preach has been borne with loving-understanding by my wife, Brenda, without whose unwavering support this work would not have been possible. Lastly, I owe special thanks to Professor Douglas Allen and T.J. MacDuff Stewart for supporting the publication of my work at Lexington Books and to Patrick Dillon for his kind editorial assistance.

Introduction

The virtuous person is a happy person, or so argue such diverse thinkers as Plato (1945), Augustine (1993) and Tenzin Gyatso, the current Dalai Lama (1999). Ethics of compassion are grounded in one's mindful commitment to one's own happiness with the recognition that the well being that one wishes for oneself also is wished for by others. Indeed, it is one's commitment to the well being of others as well as oneself that best assures a life of joy and contentment. This monograph seeks to illuminate the bases and scope of compassion ethics.

From the late 18th century, moral philosophy in the West has been split on the issue of whether "reason" is the source or ground of moral value, for example as argued for by Immanuel Kant, or whether this ground is to be found in the passional nature of human beings, for example in "sympathy" as argued for by David Hume and Adam Smith. If moral conduct is grounded in rational principles, then, it seems, moral judgments are "universalizable." This means that whatever is judged right (wrong) for me to do now is to be judged right (wrong) for any other similarly situated agent to do. On the other hand, it seems that our altruistic attitudes, such as kindness, concern and care, normally do not extend to others impartially, but are directed to those to whom we have special responsibilities in light of our relationships with them.

Ethics of Compassion follows the lead of Arthur Schopenhauer (*On the Basis of Morality*) in arguing that compassion is the source of all moral value, i.e., of "justice" and "duties of justice" as well as of other moral virtues such as loving-kindness, generosity, patience and courage. The first key to the development of this view lies in understanding the notion of "compassion" within the Buddhist context that informed Schopenhauer's analysis. Analytic philosophers writing on "compassion" often fail to recognize some of the concept's most salient dimensions largely because they do not appreciate fully how "compassion" differs from the more familiar notions of Aristotelian "pity," Humean "sympathy," and Christian "love" (*agapē*); meanwhile, the only detailed study by a scholar of Buddhism on how Buddhist ethics compares to Western theories of

1

ethics (Damien Keown's *The Nature of Buddhist Ethics*) does not mention Schopenhauer's moral theory. The second key lies in going beyond Schopenhauer's explicit analysis to show how "precepts" or "moral rules" can be derived from what Schopenhauer recognized as the two principles that all truly compassionate conduct manifests. Gerard Mannion in *Schopenhauer, Religion and Morality* speculates in a footnote, "Indeed, here I add the suggestion that Schopenhauer's method in ethics might conceivably serve as a "bridge" between Kantian ethics and modern virtue ethics." (Mannion, 2003:190) *Ethics of Compassion* aims to construct this bridge while also bridging the discourses of religious morality and normative ethical theory.

The lack of recognition of "Buddhist ethics" among Western philosophers is due primarily, I believe, to the fact that no one has set out an ethics of compassion within the framework of what Western philosophers conceive as a "normative moral theory." Such a theory should accomplish something like the following. (See Timmons, 2002:3-17)

- As a theoretical aim, provide an account of moral value that elucidates in a unified manner those fundamental features of actions, precepts and agents that make them praiseworthy or not.
- As a practical aim, provide a "decision procedure" for good moral reasoning about matters of moral concern.
- As an experiential aim, integrate into its account the culture's core moral intuitions.

A central task of *Ethics of Compassion* is to place three main elements of Mahāyāna-Buddhist ethics—compassion, precepts and the six *paramitas* ("transcendent virtues")—within the conceptual framework of normative moral theory. In doing this, I rely on Schopenhauer for direction. However, it is important to note that it is not my objective to defend Schopenhauer's presentation of his views; nor is it my aim to present Buddhist ethics as such, for this is much wider and deeper than what I have appropriated. Rather, I am indebted to Schopenhauer and to Buddhist sources for fundamentally informing and inspiring my explication of how compassion *rationally* grounds all moral value. While an emphasis on "rationality" might seem paradoxical to some who are familiar with Buddhism, in Mahāyāna Buddhism, "compassion" and "wisdom" go hand in hand with "wisdom" providing the Skillful Means (*upāya-kauśalya*) for actually benefiting beings whom one aspires to benefit. Even "spontaneous" acts of compassion, while not done by reference to "reason" or "first principles," are not acts *against* "reason" or "first principles." Indeed, an approach analogous to mine has been adopted by Western Buddhist writers intent on showing that compassion can be viewed as the ground for "human rights." (Keown, 1995a; Garfield, 1995)

I believe that it is useful for the reader to have a preview of the scope of this work and of how the various chapters fit together. The first chapter is a discussion of the Golden Rule, a principle that in one form or another is represented in most every major religious tradition. I begin with Immanuel Kant's objection to the sufficiency of the Golden Rule in providing a reliable standard of moral conduct. In recent years, philosophers have pointed out that the Golden Rule needs to be "rationalized" by a supplementary principle if it is to appropriately guide moral decisions. After discussing how philosophers have shown how the Christian and Confucian traditions offer such a supplementary principle, I provide a "rationalizing" supplementary principle from a Buddhist perspective and point out its advantages. While the notion of "compassion" is introduced here it is the central focus of Chapter II. I present a paradigmatic case of compassion from the annals of so-called "righteous gentiles" to supplement the story of the Good Samaritan. I then take a look at what contemporary Western philosophers have claimed compassion to be. Martha Nussbaum, for instance, identifies "compassion" with "pity," the emotion "at the heart" of ancient Athenian tragedy and given its "definitive analysis" by Aristotle. (Nussbaum, 1996:28) But, given that Schopenhauer was decisively influenced by the philosophies of India, it would be remarkable indeed if his concept of "compassion" is rooted in Athenian tragedy and Aristotelian ethics. Much of Chapter II is taken up with distinguishing the Buddhist-Schopenhauer concept of "compassion" from the (Aristotelian) notion of "pity" and from the Hume-Smith notion of "sympathy." While some recent analytic philosophers have nicely distinguished the concept of "compassion" from one of these other notions, no one has adequately distinguished it from both. I conclude by distinguishing compassion also from other altruistic emotions or virtues such as "care" and "kindness."

Chapter III establishes the twin principles for acting compassionately and so begins the construction of a normative theory of ethics of compassion. By joining the Golden Rule with the awareness of oneself and others as beings with a will to live without unnecessary suffering, one may rationally adopt two principles: "One ought not to cause any living being to suffer unnecessarily" and "One ought to protect/relieve living beings from unnecessary suffering." These principles are ways of understanding what Schopenhauer identified as "the supreme principle" of ethics ("Injure no one; on the contrary, help every one as much as you can"). While Schopenhauer thought that "Injure no one" constitutes the "principle of justice" and "Help everyone as much as you can" is the "principle of loving kindness," I show how Schopenhauer's reasoning actually explains how the two principles underlie the meaning of acting "justly" (or doing what is "right"). "Compassion" and "justice" are two ways of looking at the morality of conduct, the first from the perspective of agent-intention and the second from the perspective of what is "justifiable." This enables us to overcome Lawrence Blum's contention that "compassion" and "duty" are distinct and incompatible sources of moral value and that our moral nature is "bifurcated." On the contrary, compassion can serve as the *rational* ground of all truly moral conduct. I conclude Chapter III with an appendix on how an ethic of compassion might relate to Jesus' Parable of The Laborers in the Vineyard.

The key to acting compassionately is in the development of one's capacities to affectively understand one's own and (so) others' vulnerabilities to suffering. Out of this understanding, one learns how to "apply" the principles of compassion; first to see what general "precepts" are grounded on those principles and, second, to deepen one's view on how to practice those precepts. Whereas Schopenhauer does not attempt to deduce precepts or rules from his supreme principle(s), the Mahāyāna Buddhist tradition commonly asserts five basic precepts of right action. The precepts have a positive ("do good") and a negative ("avoid doing evil") side and may be understood as vows one takes as "mindfulness trainings." They may be expressed (Loori, 1996:82-95) as:

- I vow to affirm life and to refrain from the taking of life
- I vow to be generous and to refrain from taking what is not given
- I vow to honor the human body and to refrain from sexual misconduct
- I vow to manifest truth and to refrain from verbal transgressions
- I vow to proceed clearly and to refrain from harmful consumption

Chapter IV considers in some detail the second ("negative") conjunct for each of the above and conceives them in terms of "ought;" e.g., "I ought to refrain from the taking of life," "I ought to refrain from taking what is not given," and so on. It does not take too much imagination to see how these "precepts for avoiding doing harm" may be derived from the principle, "I ought not to cause any living being to suffer unnecessarily." However, such proscriptions are not "absolute" precisely because situations may arise in which such conduct most likely will prevent or relieve an unnecessary suffering rather than cause an unnecessary suffering. For each of the five "negative" precepts, I provide an example of an exceptional case. Compassion ethics provides a distinctive method for determining "exceptional cases," and, furthermore, its method seems superior to those offered by standard Western moral theories, or so I argue.

Even though "principles" and "precepts" of right conduct are grounded in compassion, it still might appear that the picture of the moral life so far drawn is overly "intellectual" and does not integrate sufficiently the "emotional" and "dispositional" dimensions of human beings. In Chapter V, I examine the significance of "vices" and "virtues" to the task of moral development. First the Aristotelian view of virtue, perhaps the most dominant view in Western moral philosophy, is discussed. On this view, the virtues enable one to actualize one's human potentials within the circumstances of one's life; living virtuously enables one to flourish within the community. I then offer a contrasting view of virtue from the tradition of Mahāyāna Buddhism; here the practices of certain virtues (*paramitas*) have as their goal one's transcendence of the "self" which, in the Greek tradition, one seeks to actualize. It is crucial here to clarify the meaning of "selflessness" in relation to one's being virtuous and why one should not think that being "selfless" entails one's being "desireless" in the sense of "desire" that is essential to one's acting intentionally. All this sets the stage for linking the practice of the *paramitas* of generosity, patience/forbearance, energetic diligence, meditation and wisdom with the "positive" precepts of right action (grounded on the principle, "One ought to protect/relieve beings from unnecessary suffering") which form what I call "the responsibilities of moral aspiration." The responsibilities of moral aspiration together with those of non-harming have "universal" application and inform three broad dimensions of contemporary life in the global community: work or "right-livelihood," politics or "right-citizenship," and, lifestyle or "right-subsistence." I close Chapter V with an appendix that explains in some detail how my analysis of "selflessness" is in keeping with fundamental Buddhist teachings.

Chapter VI then addresses a common and important criticism of Mahāyāna-Buddhism which applies to compassion ethics more generally, viz., the charge that the "selflessness" that being compassionate presumes is inconsistent with "agent-responsibility." This chapter begins with an Aristotelian account of agency that grounds "choice" and "responsibility" in the ongoing dispositions and character, i.e., the "selfhood," of the agent; and it then introduces the "libertarian" perspective on free will, primarily by reference to St. Augustine, Jean-Paul Sartre and Robert Kane, a contemporary American philosopher. Against this background, I then develop an original account of "free rational choices" that provides an appropriate basis for ascriptions of agent-responsibility without presupposing either "The Real Self View" or "The Autonomy View" of moral agents. Rather, I advance an amended version of "The Reason View" developed by Susan Wolf. In short, it is the capacity for "free rational choices" that grounds agent-responsibility. I then go on to explain how "agent-accountability," "praise," "blame," and "punishment" function within the parameters of compassionate intentionality.

The concluding Postscript indicates that ethics of compassion are indeed rooted in a tension between one's conceiving oneself as a concrete individual with one's "own" dispositions, desires and goals and as a being fundamentally inter-connected with and capable of selfless concern for others. This tension is not at odds with one's being a morally responsible person; rather it guides one in realizing a life of happiness for oneself and others.

In sum, *Ethics of Compassion* offers a perspective on morality presented as rationally humanistic and consonant with spiritual insight; and it engages and attempts to account for "core moral intuitions," likely shared by the reader, rooted in important religious teachings and in widely known theoretical principles and analyses advanced by philosophers. For readers who are not so concerned with the more technical issues addressed, they may pass over the chapter appendices as well as Chapter VI.3-4 without interrupting the flow of presentation on the nature and scope of compassion ethics.

Chapter I
Golden Rule Reasoning

> Tradition—the collective wisdom of my greatest forerunners—tells me that I should do unto others as I would that they should do unto me. My reason shows me that only by all acting thus is the highest happiness for all men attained. Only when I yield myself to that intuition of love which demands obedience to this law is my own heart happy and at rest.
>
> Tolstoy, "Letter to Ernest Howard Crosby"

In the broadest sense "the Golden Rule" is the notion that one's own desires can serve, by analogy, as a standard for how one is to treat others. This notion can be formulated either positively or negatively. For instance, the most well known formulation in the Christian tradition is: "as you wish that men would do to you, do so to them" (*Luke*, 6:31; cf. *Matthew*, 7:12); whereas the Confucian tradition emphasizes the negative formulation: "What you do not want done to yourself, do not do to others." (*Analects*, 15.23/24; 12.2)

In one form or other, the Golden Rule functions in most of the world's great religions and it is embedded in the ethics of Plato and Aristotle as well.[1] It seems that some version of the Golden Rule is invoked whenever human beings reflect systematically on the nature of right conduct. Exploring how the Golden Rule might provide a criterion for moral judgment offers insight into the nature of sympathy which lies at the foundation of altruistic intention which is the foundation of an ethic of compassion.

In this chapter, first I review Immanuel Kant's "rejection" of the Golden Rule as an adequate standard for moral judgment and why, as recent writers have shown, the Golden Rule needs to be "rationalized" by a supplementary principle if it is to provide such a standard. Secondly, I look at how the Christian and Confucian traditions generate quite distinct "supplementary" principles to the Golden Rule--principles that ground the notion of "right conduct." Thirdly, I develop a rationalized Golden Rule within a Buddhist-oriented framework and indicate its superiority to alternative constructions of the Golden Rule as well as to Kant's own alternative principle, the Categorical Imperative.

1. Kant's Challenge to the Golden Rule

Western philosophers generally see the Golden Rule as an "imperative" that prescribes how one ought or ought not to behave. As Alan Gewirth (1978) puts it:

> Thus the Golden Rule sets forth a criterion of the moral rightness on inter-personal actions or transactions. This criterion consists in the agent's desires or wishes for himself *qua* recipient: what determines the moral rightness of a transaction initiated or controlled by some person is whether he would himself want to undergo such a transaction at the hand of other persons. (Gewirth, 1978:13)

Despite its pedigree, the Golden Rule, understood as providing a criterion or standard sufficient for moral discernment, has been dismissed by Western philosophers since Kant. In a well-known footnote to the *Groundwork of the Metaphysics of Morals*, Kant claims of the Golden Rule:

> It can be no universal law because it contains the ground neither of duties to oneself nor of duties of love to others (for many a man would gladly agree that others should not benefit him if only he might be excused from showing them beneficence), and, finally it does not contain the ground of duties owed to others; for a criminal would argue on this ground against the judge punishing him, and so forth. (Kant, 1996a:80n)

Even if one is skeptical of Kant's notion of "duties to oneself," it remains true that many people have very diminished views of themselves and how they wish themselves to be treated; and, clearly, condoning treatment to oneself that goes against one's own long-term good surely should not give one the "right" to similarly treat another person. Put otherwise, "the agent's wishes for himself *qua* recipient may not be in accord with his recipient's own wishes as to how he is to be treated" (Gewirth, 1978:133). Moreover, as with Kant's criminal, what one might wish for oneself might go against justified social rules or practices; what then? This so-called "particular interpretation," according to which it is an agent's particular wishes or desires that are to serve as standards of conduct towards others, has received near unanimous rejection.[2]

However, there is also a "general interpretation" of the Golden Rule that some Western philosophers endorse. On this view, as expressed by Marcus Singer, "I am to treat others *as* I would have them treat me, that is on the same principle or standard as I would have them apply in their treatment of me." (Singer, 1963:300) If the Golden Rule, under such a general interpretation, is meant to be a necessary and sufficient condition for the acceptability of "principles or standards" of morally "right" or "permissible" conduct, then it too fails.

In so far as the Golden Rule provides a principle of consistency or "universalizability" in moral reasoning, then it yields, at best, "fairness" but not "rightness." R.M. Hare famously argued that the principled Nazi must wish that he would suffer the same fate as Jews, i.e., extermination, if it were to come to light, say, that one of his grandparents was a Jew. If a Nazi could will the Jews' outcome for himself (if the roles were "reversed") then, according to Hare, this demonstrates his "fanaticism;" but, nevertheless, he is acting according to the Golden Rule and, so, according to ethical principle—however deficient or false that principle may be! Hare's example rather shows that to act "on principle" is necessary but not sufficient to act on a justifiable "moral principle."[3]

It seems then that the Golden Rule needs to be supplemented if it is to be a standard for moral conduct. Gewirth suggests that the Golden Rule be "rationalized" to read: "Do unto others as you would rationally want them to do unto you." Interestingly, Gewirth shows that this formulation is equivalent to: "Do unto others as you have a right that they do unto you." (Gewirth, 1978:141-43) Since rationally one would wish for whatever is necessary for one to be a purposive agent, then if "freedom" and "well-being" are so necessary (as Gewirth claims), it is sensible to say that one has a "right" to them. This strategy responds effectively to the sort of concerns raised by Kant; for instance, "every person insofar as he is rational must desire that he be the recipient of . . . superogatory actions in relevant circumstances; hence, according to the Rational Golden Rule, it is right or fitting that he performs such actions towards others." (Gewirth, 1978:145)

The Rational Golden Rule does not allow one to generate standards of conduct solely from one's own desires *qua* recipient, since, rationally, just as one would want others to respect her *own* freedom and well-being, so one must be willing to respect the *other's* freedom and well-being; and this often requires, as we shall see, that one act towards another differently than how one would like oneself to be treated if one were in the other's situation.

2. Rationalizing the Golden Rule in the Christian and Confucian Traditions

Jeffrey Wattles, an important commentator on the Golden Rule speaking from the Christian tradition, emphasizes the point, "Counterexamples will only harass the rule if it is abstracted from every context, taken literally, and made to function as a necessary or sufficient condition for sound moral judgment or as the sole normative axiom in a system of ethics." (Wattles, 1996:139) In an earlier article, Wattles cites the "context" within which Matthew presents Jesus' teaching of the Golden Rule: "Here the rule of how to treat others is juxtaposed with the teaching of how God treats us. It is as though our treatment of others were to be like an answer to a prayer." (Wattles, 1987:122) Commentators often identify Jesus' teaching of the Golden Rule with the commandment, "Love thy neighbor as thyself." Wattles views the commandment to love others within the context of the Christian revelation of the nature of divine love: "Jesus made the rule more concrete when he said, 'Love one another as I have loved you' (*John,* 14:34)." (Wattles, 1987:113) If one sees oneself primarily as a son or daughter of God, then it is as God's son or daughter that one would like to be treated; and, naturally, the model of such treatment is God's way of loving us. The highest level of meaning of the Golden Rule, at least within the Christian tradition, therefore is understood by Wattles to be: "Do to others as God wants you to do to them." (Wattles, 1987:111f) [4]

As the Golden Rule is thought to express the "law of love" in the Christian tradition, it often is thought to express "considerability" (or "altruistic concern") in the Confucian tradition.[5] The Confucian understanding of the Golden Rule consists of two notions—*chung* and *shu*—which largely comprise the "one thread" of the Way of the *Analects. Shu* denotes a kind of "fellow feeling" or "consideration" for others that emerges from placing oneself in the other's position. It is *shu* that commentators identify with the negative formulation of the Golden Rule; but recognizing that I should not fail to give to another that consideration with which I would like to be treated, does not in itself inform me of how I specifically should act in a given situation. As Fingarette observes: "*shu* gives me no guidance . . . as to what specific values I should invoke in making my ultimate judgment." (Fingarette, 1979:387) So, *shu* needs to be supplemented by *chung* or "loyalty" to (the integrity of) individual persons in ways that embody *li,* the "ritual" practices that are culturally rooted within the "hearts/minds" of the members of a community. (Wang, 1999:420) The spirit of *li* grounds one's own integrity and commitments to others as members of the community. In the *Analects*:

> we are told: '*chu chung-hsin,*' and 'always follow *shu.*' Expanded this may be read: Let there always be good faith and loyalty of one person to another, as specified for varying circumstances and persons by the *li*; and let this always be conditioned by direct analogizing of self with other, rather than being solely a matter of conventions and rules and law. (Fingarette, 1979:397)

The Confucian Golden Rule, then, may be summarized this way: *shu* as the governor of *chung* is the method of (cultivating) *jen,* "humaneness." (Ivanhoe, 1990:26-27) It works roughly as follows. With regard to one's superiors (and equals), one acts according to ritualistic propriety as one would want or hope, as a superior (or equal), to be treated; here one would tend to act with utmost mindfulness of what propriety strictly requires as one would wish inferiors to act toward oneself. However, placing oneself in the positions of one's inferiors, and understanding the issues they face, one should not demand from them perfect compliance or loyalty to *li.* Taken together, following the Golden Rule expresses "considerability" and fosters humaneness first by not demanding or expecting all that one might be due from an inferior; and, second, by inspiring one to give to the superior (or equal) a perfected loyalty over and above what the superior might demand but which, nevertheless, would be appropriate and pleasing.

Nivison summarizes Confucius' teaching this way: "The Chinese Golden Rule as here stated—and so perhaps as always intended—does not say 'treat another as you would have that other treat you,' but 'treat another as you would have anyone else related to you as you are to that other treat you.'" (Nivison, 1996:65) To take an example from our own culture, suppose that after recently relocating to a distant city, you were invited to a neighbor's home for a formal dinner party with other neighbors. The evening was splendid, the hosts were gracious, the dinner was elegant, and the neighbors all welcoming and friendly. In deciding how to respond appropriately, e.g., whether it is really necessary to send a written note of thanks or to reciprocate by offering the hosts your hospitality, you should ask yourself, "What would I as a gracious host understand propriety to expect of a sincerely appreciative guest?," and act accordingly.

It might seem that the Christian commitment to "love one's neighbor" and the Confucian commitment to *li* would imply that the Golden Rule operates, in both cases, within a community of shared faith (loyalty) and practices. For this reason, the story of the Good Samaritan challenges one understandings of how the Golden Rule is to be understood or applied from both the Christian and the Confucian perspectives. Recall that on the matter, "Who is my neighbor?," Jesus responds:

> A man was going down from Jerusalem to Jericho, and he fell among robbers, who stripped him and beat him, and departed, leaving him half dead. Now by chance a priest was going down that road; and when he saw him he passed by on the other side. So likewise a Levite, when he came to the place and saw him, passed on the other side. But a Samaritan, as he journeyed, came to where he was; and when he saw him, he had compassion, and went to him and bound up his wounds, pouring on oil and wine; then he set him on his own beast and brought him to an inn, and took care of him. . . . Which of these three, do you think, proved neighbor to the man who fell among the robbers? (*Luke*, 10:30-36)

The Hebrew priest's passing by, on some accounts, is due to the uncleanness of the battered traveler (also a Hebrew) and the priest's duty to maintain ritual purity. This sort of role-based "morality" is what Jesus' teaching of the Golden Rule seems intended to counteract. Should we not treat even the outsider, the stranger, as a "neighbor," particularly when he or she is close at hand? But, still, what does it mean to treat the other as one would wish to be treated? Following Kant's first counter-example, one might suppose that many a man would not want an "other"—e.g., an "outsider"—to assist him if only he would not be obligated to assist an "other." To this the Christian has a ready reply: In God's eyes, there are no "we" and "others;" being all sons and daughters of God, we should treat everyone as we would wish to be treated as God's son or daughter; we should love others as God loves us; we should do unto others as God would want us to do. The teaching of this story precisely is that "being a Good Samaritan" to others, even strangers, is what God/Jesus wants us to do.

Let us now turn to the question of how the Confucian understanding of the Golden Rule is to apply to the case of the Good Samaritan. At first it might seem that the priest's passing by would be consistent with our analysis of how *shu* governs *chung*; for, if the priest puts himself in the place of the battered stranger, he might reason, "For me, an Uncleaned one, to want a priest to render aid would mean that I am willing to defile a priest and that would bring to me more harm than benefit; I better wait to see who else might come by." On the other hand, since the Samaritan is not a member of the Hebrew community, to what *li* might *chung* make reference in his reasoning? The Confucian practice of the Golden Rule provides for considerability within a shared social framework, and, so, has particular applicability in situations similar to Kant's second counter-example of the prisoner pleading the judge, as we shall see. But can it apply between people of distinct cultures? Indeed, Professor Quingjie James Wang insists that the virtue of the Confucian Golden Rule is that it yields "communalizability" rather than "universalizability," the latter being an illusion born of an alleged "transcendent" moral authority addressing "pure consciousnesses" rather than being rooted in the flesh and blood experience of human beings. (Wang, 1999:426ff)[6]

In sum, the Christian Golden Rule seems particularly apt for situations in which we relate to others *qua* human beings. On the other hand, within the context of social life defined by *li*, we do not relate to others simply *qua* human beings, but precisely in light of our social relationships and roles, and here the deployment of the Confucian Golden Rule has remarkable power in clarifying right conduct.

3. A Buddhist-Oriented View of the Golden Rule

A foundational moral concept for the Buddhist is "compassion," the central focus of Chapter 2. Here I merely introduce this concept through several verses of Shantideva's *Bodhicharyavatara* or *The Way of the Bodhisattva* (1997), composed in the early eighth century in Northern India.

> Just as I defend myself
> From all unpleasant happenings, however small,
> Likewise I shall act for others' sake
> To guard and shield them with compassion. (8.110)

The essential insight here is that each of us desires to be free from suffering and that if one can identify with the other, one will act to relieve another's suffering as one would one's own.

> Likewise, different beings in their joys and sorrows,
> Are, like me, all one in wanting happiness.
>
> My pain does not in fact afflict
> Or cause discomfort to another's body.
> Through clinging to my "I," this suffering is mine.
> And, being mine, is very hard to bear.

And other beings' pain
I do not feel, and yet
Because I take them for my own
Their suffering is likewise hard to bear.

And therefore I'll dispel the pain of others,
For it is simply pain, just as my own.
And others I will aid and benefit,
For they are living beings, just like me. (8.91-94)

Since I and other beings both,
In fleeing suffering, are equal and alike,
What difference is there to distinguish us,
That I should strive to save myself and not the other? (8.96)

(Shantideva, 1997:123)

On this view, it is not simply "how one would wish to be treated" that establishes the ground of acting towards others (or even towards oneself), but rather it is one's desire to avoid unnecessary suffering that establishes this ground. Just as I would not want others to cause me suffering (not necessary for my benefit) I ought not to cause others to so suffer. Just as I would wish to be relieved from pain and suffering, so too should I relieve others from their pains and sufferings. Notice too that this formulation is not subjective in the sense that it presumes that what brings suffering to others is what brings suffering to oneself. As we will see in detail in Chapter II, to be compassionate is to identify with the sufferings of others and to strive with others for their alleviation.

Despite its deep similarities with other traditions, I think that there are important advantages to a Buddhist-oriented perspective on the Golden Rule. The first follows from the fact that the applicable supplementary principle, explicated in Chapter III, "Living beings have a will to live and to prosper and to avoid unnecessary suffering," is of a kind quite distinct from those operating within the Christian and Confucian traditions. It does not specify directly what "right actions" are; rather it is a statement about the nature of living beings, one that is widely subscribed to on grounds independent of metaethical issues.[7] Unlike a principle such as "Do to others as what God wants you to do to them," it is not a general principle that has the effect of defining "right action" in a way that makes the Golden Rule superfluous. And, unlike the Confucian principle that "right action" is defined by reference to (the spirit of) *li*, it has application cross culturally (and cross species).

To illustrate this first advantage, we might consider again Kant's second counter-example of the prisoner pleading the judge. It is instructive to note that the Golden Rule is not what Kant's criminal example seems to suppose, viz., "Do unto another as that other would wish be done unto him;" in any case, basing a standard of conduct on the particular desires of the recipient would have the same weakness as basing a standard on the particular desires of the agent. Obviously the judge is not morally obliged to treat the defendant simply as the defendant may wish to be treated, particularly since the defendant may not have any genuine commitment to the political-legal practices that define his situation. Suppose the judge were to think, "In the defendant's shoes, I would wish to be set free from any legal sanction, even though there is no doubt that I have been fairly found to have violated a perfectly just law." In this case, we might say that the judge would be hypocritical in punishing the defendant since his loyalty to the system of justice he is entrusted to serve is compromised by partiality (towards himself here, but perhaps such partiality would extend to family, friends, and so on). Even so, as Kant saw, the judge would not be acting wrongly by virtue of acting hypocritically. Suppose instead that the judge reasons, "If I were this defendant I would wish to be punished 'fairly' (or 'justly' or 'mercifully')." But how are these concepts to be understood? Clearly, *qua* judge, one's understanding of such concepts is not with the mind of God, but rather, at best, within a well conceived practice or tradition of jurisprudence. The judge, then, should act out of loyalty to the values embedded in the practices of jurisprudence, which is precisely what the Confucian understanding of the Golden Rule recommends. The Confucian Golden Rule, then, works well on the presumption that the values embedded in the judicial norms and practices deserve one's respect, one's loyalty.

Similarly, the Christian Golden Rule, as interpreted through Wattles' secondary principle, "Do to others as God wants you to do to them," historically shares the same presumption. This is so based on the view that God has established state authority (*Romans* 13) and, so, the laws of the state reflect divine will.[8]

However, the Buddhist-oriented view does not endow *de facto* norms and practices with moral authority, and, so, Kant's example poses this question: does the judicial system operate in the most compassionate way possible in relieving/protecting beings from suffering? Does the judicial system both protect the community and serve to rehabilitate the offender (which would render punishment as a necessary suffering for the overall good of the offender as well as of the community)? For, if one cannot answer these questions positively, should not one refuse to assume the position of judge and so place oneself in the situation of being a moral hypocrite? Or, suppose that Kant's "criminal" in fact is innocent, though was found to be guilty; suppose further that the judge realizes this since certain evidence that was legally impermissible to present in court is in fact exculpatory. Might not the judge, were he this defendant, wish to be released from a sentence of harsh punishment, not withstanding his commitment to the rule of law? Should not the judge work real justice in this case? Does it not remain true that however one is to regard others *qua* human (sentient) beings, that is how one is to treat them, regardless of the social "roles"ll one may assume?

The second advantage of the Buddhist-oriented view is that it recognizes that the impulse to do good (reflected in "Do unto others . . . ") extends to all human beings as well as to sentient beings generally. Leslie Mulholland provides a provocative response to the question, "Who are the others? or who is my neighbor." She first notes that the Golden Rule, within the Christian tradition, does not mean that we are to love all others equally.

We are not to love God as ourselves—we must rather love God much more. While we are to love our neighbours as ourselves, we are to love God with all our hearts, minds, strength, etc. We are not expected to love our neighbour with such totality. Moreover, we are informed that we are better than creatures such as sparrows and fish. We are not expected to treat them as we would ourselves be treated. We are allowed, for instance, to eat fish. But who would want to be eaten by a shark? (Mulholland, 1988:89-90)

What is instructive here, for our purposes, is the common presumption that the "others" ("neighbors") with respect to whom the Golden Rule applies, are one's "equals." This might go back to Aristotle, who reserved unqualified Golden Rule consideration for "friends" while also holding that true friendship is grounded on love between equals. (*Nic. Eth.*, 1172a32-33; Cf., Wattles, 1996:37f.) Mulholland takes Kant to have suggested that "a being is my neighbor and a moral equal if he is able to obligate me morally reciprocally with my capacity to obligate him." (Mulholland, 1988:93) If we take Kant's Categorical Imperative to be a rationalized Golden Rule, then we can agree with the point Mulholland makes: "In effect Kant identifies two factors that determine who the others are in the application of the golden rule [*sic*: Categorical Imperative]. First, the others must be rational beings, secondly they must be sympathetically related to oneself. That is, one must be able to imagine oneself in their position." Further, "to imagine oneself in another's position" means, for Mulholland, that "[the] other must be one whose position is a real possibility for ourselves, and thus within the scope of natural possibility." (Mulholland, 1988:93)

Surely, this view yields absurd results. As Adam Smith observed over two hundred years ago, it is quite possible for a man to sympathetically share in the sufferings of a woman giving birth, without thinking that this is a real possibility for him! (Smith, 1969:466) The Confucian application of the Golden Rule requires precisely that one "identify" with the positions of others, whether "superiors" or "inferiors," and this too does not mean that there is a "real" ("natural") possibility of actually reversing roles with or obligating similarly (all of) the others to whom one is relating. While one who is subject to the Golden Rule, by adopting it as a standard of conduct, *ipso facto* is a "moral agent," this does not entail that only "other moral agents" are to be treated in accordance with it. Moral considerability is independent of moral agency, let alone "moral equality." To treat another being "equally" to oneself, does not presume that the other is "equivalent" to oneself in capacities, but to recognize that it is vulnerable to suffering, as is oneself, and to treat it "impartially," that is, with the same respect for well being that one would wish for oneself (and/or for some other being for whom one cares the most).[9]

We may grant Kant's main contention that the Golden Rule in and of itself does not provide a sound criterion for distinguishing "right" from "wrong" conduct. As we have seen, the Golden Rule needs to be "rationalized" by a supplementary principle, and different religious traditions offer quite distinctive supplementary principles. We shall see in detail how an ethic of compassion permits our acting towards others in socially acceptable and morally honorable ways with the spirit of considerability that Confucius so profoundly articulated, and, in addition, it allows for cross-cultural recognition of the sufferings of others as calling forth, making claims on, our humane concern, as in the case of the Good Samaritan. Moreover, compassion legitimately extends to all sentient beings liable to states of suffering. In Chapter II we will seek to clarify the nature of compassion so that in Chapter III we might understand how it provides the ground for all moral value. Only then can we return to Kant to offer a detailed criticism of the distinction he draws between "perfect" and "imperfect" duties in light of the respect one owes to oneself and others as human beings.

4. Appendix: Golden Rule Reasoning in Everyday Life

We have reviewed briefly how the Golden Rule might be practiced within three distinct spiritual traditions. The common starting point is to (not) treat others as one would wish (not) to be treated. In the Christian tradition, one is to see oneself and others as sons and daughters of God, and to wish for oneself and others to be treated as God (Jesus) would treat us. In the Confucian tradition, one is to see oneself and others within the fabric of mutual relationships, and to wish for oneself and others to be treated in accordance with *li*, the practices that root our humanity. And in the Buddhist tradition, one is to see oneself and others as suffering beings, and to wish for oneself and others the protection against suffering that a loving mother would provide to her endangered child. One question (to pursue in discussion) is: in concrete situations, how similarly would one treat other human beings out of Christian "love," Confucian "considerateness," and Buddhist "compassion?"

Indeed, descriptions of Golden Rule reasoning in the West often integrate elements from each of the three traditions we have reviewed. Consider the celebrated case of Arthur Nash who (along with JC Penney) famously applied the Golden Rule in the development of an exceptionally successful business enterprise. At the end of WW I, early in his career of making made-to-order suits, Nash took over a teetering sweatshop operation that leased space in his building. The idea was to close up the operation in several months, but Nash wanted to pay the workers a living wage until then. He provides this account of how he went to his workers to announce this decision.

'First, I want you to know that Brotherhood is a reality with me. You are my brothers and sisters, children of the same great Father that I am, and entitled to all the justice and fair treatment that I want for myself. And so long as we run this shop [which for me meant three or four months longer], God being my helper, I am going to treat you as my brothers and sisters, and the Golden Rule is going to be our governing law. Which means that whatever I would like you to do to me, were I in your place, I am going to do to you. Now,' I went on, 'not knowing any of you personally, I would like you to raise your hands as I call your names.' I read the first name. Under it was written: Sewing on buttons--$4.00 per week. I looked straight before me at the little group, but saw no hand. Then I looked to my right, and there saw the old lady I have referred to holding up her trembling hand. At first I could not speak, because, almost instantly, the face of my own mother came between that old lady and myself. I thought of my mother being in that situation, and of what, in the circumstances, I would want someone to do for her. . . . But as I looked at that old lady, and saw only my mother, I finally blurted out: 'I don't know what it's worth to sew on buttons; I never sewed a button on. But your wages, to begin with, will be $12.00 a week.' (From Wattles, 1996:98-99)

Nash then raised the wages of all of the least paid workers by 300 percent and the wages of the highest paid workers by 50 percent, all the while realizing that much of these expenditures likely would come out of his pocket at considerable sacrifice to his family. After several months had passed, Nash was surprised to learn that this little operation was three times as productive compared to the previous year.

He then learned that after his little speech the Italian presser had concluded that if he were the boss and had just spoken like that to his employees and raised their wages, he would want his employees to 'work like hell.' And that is exactly what they did .. . . Encouraged, Nash turned his business into laboratory for the application of the golden rule, and the business prospered greatly. (Wattles, 1996:99)

While it is common to associate the Golden Rule with how one should treat "anyone," even strangers, in fact we do not relate to others as abstract, separate(d) beings; nor do we act towards them as we would like ourselves, as independent beings, to be treated. The Italian presser does not see his commitment to his boss in terms of what he *qua* individual human being owes to another human being; nor of what he *qua* worker owes to another *qua* boss; nor even in terms of what he as "any boss" would expect from "any worker." Rather, he is mindful of the considerateness of *his* boss, and of what kind of treatment, were he *that* boss, he would wish for himself. Similarly, Nash did not respond to "the old woman" as to "any old woman;" nor, did he place himself in her situation to determine how he would like to be treated, were he she. Rather, he related to the old woman as he would wish his own mother to be treated; that is, as he would treat the person for whom he most cared. Even though he proclaims his commitment to the Golden Rule in terms of how he relates to others as "brothers and sisters," and that he will treat them as if he were they, his responsiveness to others seems more indicative of how the Buddhist might "exchange self and others." In sum, in concrete situations, the Golden Rule is practiced not in accordance with any one "meaning" but with a richness and complexity that spans narrow, traditional formulations. Stated differently, each of the traditions we have surveyed manifest various ways in which one may seek to become "One who sees all beings in one's self and one's self in all beings." (Cf. Wattles, 1996:112; taken from a teaching attributed to the Upanishads) And in so doing, one's own love/considerateness/compassion evokes kind-heartedness in others who may do to others as is done to them if not as they might wish be done to them.

Notes

1. For a listing of such references see Gewirth, 1978:146, fn 1. Jeffrey Wattles' book, *The Golden Rule* (1996), is the most extensive, accessible treatment of the topic I know and it includes a helpful bibliography. In his introduction, Wattles remarks:

> Despite the fact the golden rule is expressed, in some form, in most or all of the world's religions, only in the Confucian and Judeo-Christian traditions did the rule become a prominent theme for sustained reflection. . . . That the focus of the book is thus limited does not imply that the virtues symbolized by the golden rule are any less present in traditions such as Hinduism and Buddhism that are not discussed here. (Wattles, 1996:9)

Indeed, that Buddhism embraces "the virtues symbolized by the golden rule" is due to its reflective appropriation of the rule itself, as indicated later in this chapter.

2. Gould (1983) offers a perceptive defense of Kant's view. Singer (1963) dismisses the particular interpretation of the Golden Rule as do (among others) Gewirth (1978), Fingarette (1979), Wattles (1987), and, most recently, Trapp (1998).

3. R.M. Hare, 1965, Ch. 9. According to Wattles (1996:137), "[Harry] Gensler relates a report of an actual case of a Nazi who, upon discovering that he had Jewish ancestry, arranged for himself and his family to be put in concentration camps and killed." We might say that here one's unwillingness to "respect" the "outside-other's" human rights and interests becomes "internalized" and, as a result, one denies one's own humanity.

4. In *Luke* (6:36) the statement of the Golden Rule is soon followed by "Be merciful even as your Father is merciful." "Love thy neighbor as thyself" follows the greater commandment to love God with one's whole heart, mind and soul. It is in loving God whole-heartedly that Christians (hope to) establish their will in God (or, that God's will is established them) so that one then acts with the mercy of God or as God wills one to act. Hans Kung, after noting how the Commandment, for Luke, holds for enemies, observes:

> God can be rightly understood only as the Father who makes no distinction between friend and foe, who lets the sun shine and the rain fall on good and bad, who bestows his love even on the unworthy (and who is not unworthy?). Through love human beings are to prove themselves sons and daughters of this Father and become brothers and sisters [even] after being enemies. God's love for all men is for me then the reason for loving the person whom he sends to me, for loving just this neighbor. (Kung, 1976:220)

5. Ivanhoe, 1990:17. Over the past two decades there has appeared an insightful series of essays analyzing and comparing the Christian and Confucian understandings of the Golden Rule. (Fingarette, 1979; Allinson, 1985; Ivanhoe, 1990; Nivison, 1996: Wattles, 1996:Ch. 2; and Wang, 1999) Here I will not attempt to capture, let alone evaluate, the profoundly rich and intricately textured strands of analyses that have been offered. I should point out, however, that Fingarette illuminates instructive parallels between the twofold ground of the Golden Rule in both traditions; also he sees "the one thread" as weaving throughout a broader set of concepts than do many of his successors. In any case, my aim simply is to show how both Jesus and Confucius presuppose a certain context within which their proclamation of the Golden Rule acquires a more definite meaning than what might otherwise be supposed; in showing this I appeal to relatively common ground among scholarly interpreters. My objective is not to

argue for a particular scholarly interpretation of either the Christian or the Confucian teaching, but to show how the Buddhist understanding of the Golden Rule is quite distinct and, perhaps, more fruitful for contemporary purposes.

6. Robert Allinson (1992) claims to discern a teaching of "universal love" in Confucius. His analysis presumes both that *shu* is a negative formulation of the Golden Rule and is not expressible in a positive form and that *shu* is not in need of *chung*; from this the paradoxical result follows that *shu* "does not counsel us to take action towards others." This interpretation is unpersuasive. At most, one might take the *Analects* as preparation for the complete cultivation of character: just as the practice of filial piety by a young person enables that person, when older, to act with consideration for others generally, so, too, the latter practice (i.e., following the Golden Rule), if perfected, leads to, or enables one to be, *jen*.

7. While the recognition that all beings wish to be happy grounds compassion towards others, it also reinforces the view that it is natural for one to desire happiness for oneself and that one should be compassionate towards oneself as well as to others. This recognition is fundamental to the training of Mahāyāna Buddhists, at least in the Tibetan-Buddhist tradition. B. Alan Wallace recounts:

> Many hundreds of discourses on Dharma that I have heard from Tibetans have begun with the statement that every sentient being seeks happiness, and seeks to be free from suffering. Such a simple truth. Yet it's worth bringing front and center. Every single sentient being wishes to be happy and free of suffering. By no means does Buddhism say this is wrong; rather, this is where we start from. (Wallace, 1999:89)

8. The Christian might hold that de facto legal/political authority expresses God's will and, so, to do what is legally prescribed is to act towards others as God would wish one to. But, as Augustine famously declared, "An unjust law is no law at all." (Augustine, 1993:8) When Wattles (1987) offers the principle, "Do to others what God wants you to do to them," he is combining the commandments to "love God" and "love neighbor" into one principle, with clear priority to the commandment to love God. It seems though that this might yield unwelcomed outcomes. Suppose, one interprets "God's will" as requiring that we treat one another "justly" and that one holds to a "retributivist" view on the belief that this view is endorsed by God. The result might then be that one would sanction the killing of a murderer or the waging of war against an "unjust" state. But, could one really wish that he be subject as a criminal offender or the enemy combatant to the willful taking of his life? How does the Golden Rule as expressing "love of neighbor" provide grounds for such conduct? Fingarette (1979:392) interestingly suggests that the Christian Golden Rule is best thought of in terms of one's integrating the two commandments into one's decision as to how to act in the given circumstances rather than into a single principle to cover all act-decisions. What this means is that in acting, one must treat another as he genuinely would wish to be treated *and* in doing so act out of love of God and out of God's love for man. Here, the Golden Rule functions to limit what one might accept as truly being "God's will."

9. This issue is addressed further in Chapters II and V. A third advantage of the Buddhist-oriented perspective is that it recognizes both the negative and the positive formulations of the Golden Rule, without the quite dubious presumption that the two are "equivalent" or that one formulation is "superior" to the other. The proposed analysis does see the negative formulation as being more basic in that it is more incumbent upon one generally to "avoid doing evil" than to "do good," for reasons discussed in Chapter III. There just is not a persuasive account for

why one who would consent to one formulation would not also consent to the other, even if they are not equivalent.

Chapter II
"Compassion" and Related Notions

Compassion is a far greater and nobler thing than pity. Pity has its roots in fear and carries a sense of arrogance and condescension, some times even smug feeling of 'I'm glad it's not me.' As Stephen Levine says: 'When your fear touches someone's pain it becomes pity; when your love touches someone's pain it becomes compassion.' To train in compassion is to know that all beings are the same and suffer in similar ways, to honor those who suffer, and to know that you are neither separate from nor superior to anyone.

Sogyal Rinpoche, *The Tibetan Book of Living and Dying*

In a recent article, Charles Taylor relates the story of Samuel and Pearl Oliner, a couple who were honored as "Righteous Gentiles" for their rescue of many Jews during their persecution in Nazi Europe, but who found this designation to be inappropriate

We are now called "Righteous Gentiles" or even sometimes "heroes." We much object to this title, and I can tell you why. One day there was an air raid on the German barracks near our house, some five kilometers away. My husband happened to be there. . . . When it was over, the barracks were very badly hit. A German soldier came running out with his head practically destroyed. He was bleeding heavily and obviously in shock. He was running in panic. My husband saw that within minutes he would fall down and bleed to death. So my husband put him on his bicycle—without thinking about it—and brought him to the commandant's house. He put him on the step,

21

rang the bell, waited to see the door open, and left. Later some of our
friends and people who were hiding with us heard about it and said: "You
are a traitor because you helped the enemy." My husband replied: "No, the
moment the man was badly wounded, he was not an enemy any more but
simply a human being in need." As little as we would accept the title of
"traitor," so little can we accept the title of "hero" for the things we did to
help Jewish people. We just helped human beings who were in need. (Taylor, 1999:74-75)

Taylor characterizes compassion or sympathy as a "primitive response to the suffering of another" (1999:86, n15) by which he means that one's assisting the suffering
other is not mediated by reasons (or even the thought that another's suffering is a
good reason to act), but rather, in its spontaneity, expresses a constitutive element in
our conception of human nature; it is "primitive" also in the sense that it cannot be
explained empirically in terms of more fundamental categories or facts about human
beings. In thus seeing compassion as a bedrock foundation for truly moral conduct,
Taylor is expressly following in the footsteps of Arthur Schopenhauer.

Schopenhauer's *On the Basis of Morality* (1995) argues for the centrality of "the
everyday phenomenon of compassion" to understanding why and how conduct has
moral value. Compassion, on Schopenhauer's view, marks

> the immediate *participation*, independent of all ulterior consideration, primarily in
> the *suffering* of another, and thus in the prevention or elimination of it; for all satis-
> faction and well-being consists in this. It is simply and solely this compassion that is
> the real basis for all *voluntary* justice and *genuine* loving-kindness. Only in so far as
> an action has sprung from compassion does it have moral value. (Schopenhauer,
> 1995:144)

Schopenhauer not only described what compassion is but he also claimed that it is
the true basis of all moral value. This latter claim is the subject of the next chapter. In
this chapter, my aims are the more modest ones of, first, showing that Schopenhauer's conception of compassion is quite distinct from the notions of pity and sympathy, with which it is often conflated, and, second, defending Schopenhauer's conception of compassion against alternative views and misunderstandings espoused by
recent writers on the subject.

Anglo-American philosophers commonly see Aristotle as the most formative
influence in detailing the nature of compassion. One recent article opens, "Since Aristotle, compassion has been characterized as a feeling of empathy that is accompanied by a desire to enhance the fortune or reduce the misfortune of the person for
whom empathy is felt." (Brown, 1996:216) In her Gifford Lectures, Martha Nussbaum identifies "'pity' or 'compassion'" as "the emotion that lay at the heart of ancient Athenian tragedy;" its definitive analysis by Aristotle, Nussbaum claims, is
"taken over, in most respects, by a long tradition in Western philosophy—major later
exponents include both defenders of pity such as Rousseau, Schopenhauer, and

Adam Smith, and opponents of the emotion such as the ancient Stoics, Spinoza, Kant, and Nietzsche." (Nussbaum, 1996:27, 28)

On the other hand, one of analytic philosophy's most acute commentators on compassion, Lawrence Blum, claims, "Compassion has a particular cultural history: its sources are Christian, it was further developed by Romanticism, especially by the German Romantics." (Blum, 1980a:516, n1) In his insightful study of the "humanitarian" movement in Great Britain and the United States during the eighteenth century—culminating in the centrality of "sympathy" in the work of David Hume, and Adam Smith—Norman Fiering notes, "The doctrine of irresistible compassion as found in the eighteenth century was probably not more than a hundred years old." (Fiering, 1976:196)

It is not my intention here to sort out definitively the Western cultural history of compassion. But given Schopenhauer's explicit reliance on Buddhism in developing an account of moral value, we should be skeptical of claims that *his* view of compassion is rooted in Athenian tragedy or in Christianity, even if it is related to German Romanticism and its eighteenth century philosophical precedents.

1. Pity

Any philosophical analysis of the altruistic attitudes should explain how genuine concern for others is possible. Aristotle's treatment of pity is thought by some to provide the basis of an account of altruistic conduct. Now, this might surprise some since Aristotle does not discuss pity in his treatises on ethics, primarily because he sees pity only as an emotion and not as a virtue. Virtues are dispositions that "involve choice" and enable one to act well. Aristotle discusses various (other) emotions in the *Rhetoric* that are of importance to the orator who should be skilled in arousing them in his audience. For Aristotle, "The emotions are all those feelings that so change men as to affect their judgments, and that are also accompanied by pain or pleasure. Such are anger, pity, fear and the like, with their opposites." (*Rhet.*:1378a20-21) Aristotle's general method of analysis is to identify for each emotion: (a) the appropriate state of mind, (b) the types of people who are the objects of the emotion, and (c) the grounds that give rise to the emotion. (*Rhet.*:1378a23-26 and 1379a8-10) Accordingly, "Anger may be defined as an impulse, accompanied by pain, to a conspicuous revenge for a conspicuous slight directed without justification towards what concerns oneself or towards what concerns one's friends." (*Rhet.*:1378a31-33) In a similar vein: "Pity may be defined as a feeling of pain caused by the sight of some evil, destructive or painful, which befalls one who does not deserve it, and which we might expect to befall ourselves or some friend of ours, and moreover to befall us soon. (*Rhet.*:1385b12-16)

But, how does Aristotle's notion of pity resemble compassion as exemplified by Samuel Oliner and discussed by Charles Taylor? There is no reason to think that Oliner's sympathetic responsiveness to the Jews or to the German soldier involved individuals who were thought to be similar to himself or to those close to him, to be suffering from circumstances that might befall him or his loved ones soon, or, in the case of the German soldier, to be suffering an "undeserved" fate. Perhaps most tellingly, Aristotle's conception of pity omits any motivational dimension; while anger involves an impulse to avenge an undeserved wrong, pity is not said to involve an impulse to relieve an undeserved suffering.[1] Recalling the important role that "arousing pity" plays in Athenian tragedy, perhaps Aristotle thought that most often the person in whom pity is aroused, as with the theatergoer, is not in a position to render effective aid and, hence, is not motivated to altruistic conduct.

For the sake of argument, however, let us grant that the Aristotelian pitier sometimes is moved to render aid to the person who suffers undeservedly. It is the condition of "similar possibilities," to use Nussbaum's phrase, that is the most distinctive and most illuminating feature of an Aristotelian account of such behavior. On this view, pity is felt for those "close to us" or "very much like ourselves" precisely because we can imagine *ourselves* suffering their plight (or, perhaps, we find *ourselves* suffering by their plight). Nussbaum perceptively notes, "In short, the judgment of similar possibilities is part of a construct that bridges the gap between prudential concern and altruism." (1996:36) However, in the Aristotelian conceptual framework, human conduct is chosen (rationally) only if it results from a conception of something *good for oneself* (*Nic. Eth.*, VII, 3); perhaps, if one can recognize the suffering of another as something to which oneself (or loved one) is liable, and if relief from that suffering is recognized as an important good for oneself, then one would be inclined to engage in helping behavior. On the other hand, if altruistic conduct is motivated purely out of concern for another, there really is no basis for its explanation in Aristotle's analysis of pity.[2]

It is common practice for commentators to associate an attitude of condescension as integral to the emotion of pity. Interestingly, Nussbaum holds (1996:29) that this was not true for Aristotle but only surfaces in the Victorian age. Nevertheless, Aristotle's analysis of pity makes room for condescension whereas Schoperhauerian compassion does not. In Athenian tragedy, one whose serious suffering evokes pity is "befallen" in one way or another—usually attributable to a "character flaw" often in conjunction with a greater power such as "nature" or "the gods." While we all might be subject to such greater powers, the truth is that some befall misfortune and others do not; and, even if we assume that the misfortunate do not "deserve" their plight and that we are liable to similar misfortune, the fact remains that, thankfully, we are not they. I think that this is at the root of the condescension that accompanies pity. As Blum puts it:

> with the attitude characteristic of pity . . . one holds oneself apart from the afflicted person and from their suffering thinking of it as something that defines that person as fundamentally different from oneself. . . .That is why pity (unlike compassion) involves a kind of condescension. (Blum, 1980a:512)

Because of this emotional distance, the pitier, perhaps more often as not, fails to perform helping acts. An Aristotelian account, then, provides a basis for explaining both how one's "closeness" or "similarities" (in character and social position) with another *might* allow one to "identify" with the other's suffering as well as why one *might* feel condescension towards the sufferer, since it is natural to feel "superior" to a "victim" of misfortune. The pitier appears to have an empathetic understanding of another's suffering which, in itself, is insufficient to motivate helping behavior; what motivates his helping behavior, then, is not simply concern for another, but the belief that by so acting he is doing something of benefit to himself (even if that is not the relief of the pain one feels in "sharing" in "participating" in another's suffering). Moreover, once this view is fused with the Christian view that "love of neighbor" is to extend beyond those "close" to us or "like" us, the practice of "taking pity" on others yields more generalized forms of egoistic-based concern for others marked by condescension or even contempt.

How ironic indeed that the light of Schopenhauer's moral vision would be so thoroughly dimmed by the criticisms of Nietzsche. Nietzsche assumed that Schopenhauer's notion of *Mitlied* is an expression of Christian love marked with the self-centeredness and contemptuousness of the Greek notion of pity. To the contrary, Schopenhauer argued that *Mitleid* as a desire for another's well-being is possible only if another's misery becomes directly the same sort of incentive as one's own misery. Just as painful experiences contrary to my will move me in ways to relieve them, in having *Mitleid* towards another, another's misery assumes the same status as my own by moving me to relieve it.[3]

2. Sympathy

Accounting for altruistic conduct played a central role in eighteenth century British moral theory. Rather than the "empathy" characteristic of a theatergoer's "pity," attention turned to developing pity into the more complex notion of "sympathy" as the basis of altruistic conduct.

As is well known, David Hume based all voluntary conduct on "sentiment." Recognizing that pity is an "uneasiness" arising from the suffering of others and that such uneasiness naturally tends to produce hatred, Hume reasons,[4] that what allows for an altruistic response, is the operation within us of the sentiment of benevolence extended through imagination. On two counts, Hume's analysis mirrors Aristotle's: pity is "uneasiness" or "pain" arising from the suffering of another; our natural affection for those "close to us" is the basis for our extending altruistic concern to others, even strangers. Hume's explanation of this latter point is more sophisticated. "Benevolence," for Hume, denotes a desire for the happiness or well-being of those one loves. The suffering of another human being, even a stranger, can arouse in one "a feeling of uneasiness;" this feeling is enough to provoke one's taking "an interest in" the being who suffers as well as in his circumstances; this "interest" in a suffering stranger "awakens" the interest one has for loved ones, that is to say, "benevolence" or a desire for another's well-being; and, it is this desire that motivates altruistic conduct. Imagination enables one to "feel" the other's pain, by seeing oneself in the other's circumstances, and it enables one to connect the interest one has in a suffering stranger with the interest one takes in one's loved ones. While the source of one's sympathetic response lies in the affection for loved ones, Hume's account allows pity to extend more generally than does Aristotle's account since it does not require that the suffering stranger resemble in character or social position either oneself or one's loved ones. Hume's account also provides a more explicit explanation for the condescension characteristic of pity: the "uneasiness" that one feels in being aware of another's suffering can, quite readily, be directed toward or at the being whose suffering one encounters.

While Hume's analysis of pity emphasizes the role of imagination, Adam Smith provides penetrating analyses and illuminating illustrations of the imaginative "projection" or "dwelling" (to use Blum's term) that, he claims, is characteristic of "sympathy" or "fellow feeling" with another's passions generally as well as of "pity or compassion" which is the fellow-feeling for another's "sorrow."

> As we have no immediate experience of what other men feel, we can form no idea of the manner in which they are affected, but by conceiving what we ourselves should feel in the like situation. . . . By the imagination we place ourselves in his situation, we conceive ourselves enduring all the same torments, we enter as it were into his body, and become in some measure the person with him, and thus form some idea of his sensations. . . . His agonies, when they are thus brought home to ourselves, when we have thus adopted and made them our own, begin at last to affect us, and we then tremble and shudder at the thought of what he feels. (Smith, 1969:3-4)

Smith's central view is that our fellow-feelings for another's sorrow involve placing ourselves in the sufferer's circumstances in order to "form some idea of his sensations." Does imaginative projection allow us to share in the "torments" of another or does it (only) enable us to find in ourselves what we would feel if we were in the other's situation? The above passage clearly supports the latter view.

In other places, however, Smith suggests that the "imaginary change [of situations] is not supposed to happen to me in my own person and character, but that of the person with whom I sympathize." (Smith, 1969:465)

> When I condole with you for the loss of your only son, in order to enter into your grief I do not consider what I, a person of such a character and profession, should suffer, if I had a son, and if that son was unfortunately to die: but I consider what I should suffer if I was really you, and I not only change circumstances with you, but I change persons and characters. My grief, therefore, is entirely upon your account, and not the least upon my own. (Smith, 1969:466)

Here, Smith has moved seemingly from one's experiencing what he would feel if he were in another's situation to experiencing what he would feel if he were the other person in the other person's circumstances. Blum warns that this way of "identifying" with another results in a "pathological condition" harboring an "identity confusion where the compassionate person fails to distinguish his feelings and situation from the other person's." (1980a, 509) Now, one's total identification with another would account for altruistic conduct within the framework of an egoistic theory of human motivation, since to act for the well-being of another with whom one so "identifies" would then be to act for the sake of oneself. However, as illustrated by Samuel Oliner, compassionate persons normally do not suffer "an identity confusion," and, so, Smith's second account of sympathetic "identification" fails to explain everyday cases of compassionate action.[5]

3. Schopenhauer on Compassion

What Smith clearly saw is that one's "fellow-feeling" as well as the conduct it motivates are for the other and not for oneself (as a person apart from the other). Smith's analyses try to uncover the "selflessness" that characterizes truly sympathetic responsive-ness to another being. It is on this crucial point that Schopenhauer provides keen insight.

> But now how is it possible for a suffering which is not *mine* and does not touch *me* to become just as directly a motive as my own normally does, and to move me to action? As I have said, only by the fact that although it is given to me merely as something external, merely by means of external intuitive perception or knowledge, I nevertheless *feel it with him, feel it as my own*, and yet not *within me*, but *in another person*. . . . But this presupposes that to a certain extent I have identified with the other man, and in consequence the barrier between ego and non-ego is for the moment abolished; only then do the other man's affairs, his needs, distress, and suffering, directly become my own. . . . I share the suffering *in him*, in spite of the fact his skin does not enclose my nerves. Only in this way can *his* woe, *his* distress, become a motive *for me*; otherwise it can be absolutely only my own. I repeat that this *occurrence is mysterious*, for it is something our faculty of reason can give no direct account of, and its grounds cannot be discovered on the path of experience. And yet it happens everyday; everyone has often experienced it within himself; even to the most hard-hearted and selfish it is not unknown. (Schopenhauer, 1995:165-66)

Schopenhauer's analysis is magnificently nuanced and stands mid-way between Smith's two accounts just presented. For Schopenhauer, the compassionate person continuously recognizes that it is another being and not oneself that is suffering; but by sharing with another a suffering which belongs to him, i.e., characterizes *his* situation, the other's distress becomes a motive for *me*. As Schopenhauer notes, compassion involves one's identifying "to a certain extent" with another; but to say that "the barrier between ego and non-ego is for the moment abolished" does not mean that one wholly identifies with the other by assuming the other's character, that there is no distinction between oneself and another.

David Cartwright, an astute commentator, has provided the following analytical model of Schopenhauer's conception of compassion:

A has compassion for B, if and only if;

(i)   A and B are sentient creatures,

(ii) A apprehends that B is, or will be, suffering,

(iii) A participates immediately in B's suffering,

(iv) A feels grief or sorrow for B,

(v)   A desires B's well-being because B is, or will be, suffering,

(vi) A is moved to do X for B, where X is some action aimed at
      relieving B's suffering (philanthropy), or A is moved not to do Y,
      where Y is an action A has planned to perform which would cause
      B's suffering (justice).

(Cartwright, 1982:63)

Cartwright continues:

> His model of compassion is sound if we reformulate the third condition in the fol-
> lowing way: (iii)* A participates imaginatively in B's suffering. This reformulation
> of the third condition removes the need to explain the agent's participation in an-
> other's mental state metaphysically. The agent participates in the other's mental
> state by imagining how he or she would feel in the other's situation, or how he or
> she would feel in this situation if the agent had the recipient's history, personality
> temperament, etc. (Cartwright, 1982:67-68)

But to replace (iii) by (iii)* is to deny what is truly distinctive about Schopenhauer's
conception of compassion, as illustrated by the "primitive" and "immediate" nature
of Samuel Oliner's conduct, in favor of Smith's analysis.[6] Cartwright's adherence to
(iii)* follows the influential analyses of Lawrence Blum. (1980a, b) Blum characterizes the altruistic person as one who apprehends situations as involving others' "weal
and woe" and is disposed to act responsively; compassion specifically concerns conditions of woe "central to a person's life and well being, describable as pain, misery,
hardship, suffering, affliction, and the like" (1980a:508).

> Compassion is not a simple feeling-state but a complex emotional attitude toward
> another, characteristically involving imaginative dwelling on the condition of the
> other person, an active regard for his good, a view of him as a fellow human being,
> and emotional responses of a certain degree of intensity. (Blum, 1980a:509)

Blum's characterization incorporates (a) an intensity of response to a "fellow" being
that is utterly "egoless" *a la* Schopenhauer; (b) Hume's notion of regard for another's good or well-being; and (c) Smith's notion of imaginative projection.[7]

But why should Cartwright feel compelled to move in the direction of Blum and
Smith? Cartwright's underlying concern is one widely shared: if compassion is a
"feeling with" another, how is this to be explained? This question is interpreted as,
"How is it possible for one to share in or experience another's *mental states*?" After
all, if the Cartesian view is correct, then one cannot experience directly, nor share in,
another being's "mental states;" and, furthermore, if psychological egoism is correct,
then how is it that one being would take a selfless interest in the suffering of another?

These worries are misguided and to see why it will prove instructive to review once again a passage from Shantideva (1997:123) that we looked at in Chapter I:

> My pain does not in fact afflict
> Or cause discomfort to another's body.
> Through clinging to my "I," this suffering is mine.
> And, being mine, is very hard to bear.
>
> And other beings' pain
> I do not feel, and yet
> Because I take them for my own
> Their suffering is likewise hard to bear.
>
> And therefore I'll dispel the pain of others,
> For it is simply pain, just as my own.
> And others I will aid and benefit,
> For they are living beings, just like me.
>
> Since I and other beings both,
> In fleeing suffering, are equal and alike,
> What difference is there to distinguish us,
> That I should strive to save myself and not the other?

In so far as another being's "pain" signifies bodily discomfort, I do not feel that being's "pain." Yet, I can perceive that another is in pain and, by "taking it for my own," share in, and so wish to dispel, that being's suffering. Both Hume and Smith are correct to note that one can share in another's sorrow or grief (suffering); but this does not require one to (literally) "feel" the other's pain or to "form some idea of his sensations." Compassion involves the sharing of another's suffering (or distress, woe, plight) and not the sharing of another's "sensations" or "felt pains," as with Smith's standard view; and this does not require one to assume the other's circumstances *and character* as one's own, as Smith's alternative account suggests.

The heart of the matter is revealed eloquently by Max Scheler in *The Nature of Sympathy*. Scheler credits Schopenhauer for ". . . recognizing that commiseration is an 'immediate' participation in the woes of others, and does not depend on inference or on any artificial mode of 'projecting' oneself into the other person's situation." (Scheler, 1954:51) As he keenly observed, it is neither necessary nor possible to get into another's skin, as it were, to share in another's suffering.

> Hence an identical sorrow may be keenly felt (though in one's own individual fashion), but never an identical sensation of pain, for here there are always two separate sensations. Again, one may see the same shade of red as another person (without actually reducing the color to wave-motions), or hear the same sound of C. But the aural and ocular sensations involved are accessible only to the possessor of the organs in question. (Scheler, 1954:255)

Interestingly, Scheler distinguishes between these cases of "fellow-feeling."

(1) Immediate community of feeling, e.g. of one and the same sorrow, 'with someone'.
(2) Fellow-feeling 'about something'; rejoicing in his joy and commiseration with his sorrow. (Scheler, 1954:12-14)

Scheler's example of (1) is two parents standing beside the dead body of their beloved child, feeling the *same* sorrow, the *same* anguish; ". . . they feel and experience in common, not only the self-same value situation, but also the same keenness of emotion in regard to it." Their friend who joins them, however, commiserates "with them" or "with their sorrow;" this requires a sharing in *another's* sorrow, but not having it as one's own.[8]

4. Compassion: suffering-striving with another

The issues of whether and how compassion requires "imaginative in-dwelling" in another being's felt experiences have been explored in recent articles by Nancy Snow (1991, 1993) and Brian Carr (1996). Snow questions whether "imagination" is able to account for the "identification" that underlies compassion when the suffering being is non-human. Upon noting Thomas Nagel's well known point that our imagination is not up to the task of knowing what it is like for a bat to be a bat, Snow warns, "If imaginative reconstruction of another's subjective experiences is required for compassion, and if our abilities to imaginatively identify with the inner experiences of animals are limited, then it is possible to feel compassion for nonhuman animals on far fewer occasions than we think." (Snow, 1993:62-63)

On the critical issue of what is necessary in order to "identify with another's distress," Snow argues that "imaginative reconstruction" of another's suffering is not required, but rather, it is sufficient *to believe* that one is similarly vulnerable to the kind of serious misfortune that plagues the other. A cat owner might identify with her cat's plight,

> if she has the appropriate set of true and/or justified beliefs about herself and her cat. The set would include the beliefs that the cat is weak or vulnerable, that this vulnerability has occasioned some misfortune that the animal experiences, and that she is similar enough to the cat to be similarly vulnerable, and consequently liable to misfortune. (Snow, 1993:65)

However, the *belief* that one is similarly vulnerable to another being's misfortune is notoriously insufficient to generate "a suffering with" the other. This clearly is one of the lessons of the parable of The Good Samaritan. As one commentator notes: "The Samaritan, and likewise the priest and the Levite, knew *what* the battered traveler needed, and *that* they should provide assistance. It is precisely because they knew these things that the priest's and the Levite's passing by was inexcusable, while the Samaritan's actions were compassionate." (Welie, 1995:485)

What is missing in Snow's account (1993) is any foundation for how one's concern for one's own well being, e.g. the fervent wish for relief from one's own serious misfortunes, in conjunction with the recognition that the other's serious misfortune is similar to what one is likewise vulnerable, results in one's sharing in the other's plight by fervently wishing or striving (with the other, as it were) for relief from suffering.[9]

A second challenge comes from Brian Carr, who questions whether it is possible to share in "another's suffering" if the other in fact does not experience "felt suffering."

> Let us draw a distinction between the kind of suffering which is actually experienced by the sufferer, *felt suffering*, and the kind which is not, *unfelt suffering*. Examples of the latter might be a financial loss which I "suffer" but which I am unaware of; or the death of a distant relative which never comes to my attention; or a permanent comatose state which I "suffer" after an accident. There are many such cases of unfelt suffering—the list is quite easy to add to. . . . Now those who suffer but do not feel their suffering might well be candidates for *pity*, but could not be candidates for *compassion*.
>
> The reason is simply this. It is a conceptual truth that compassion involves a shared suffering, even though the degrees and kinds of suffering could be very different in the one who feels compassion and the one for whom compassion is felt. If the sufferer's suffering is unfelt . . . we can hardly 'feel with' the sufferer since the sufferer does not feel his misfortune. (Carr, 1996:420-21)

Carr clearly holds the view that sharing another's suffering (sorrow, distress) requires that one shares the "felt" mental states of another. But why cannot one share in another's "unfelt suffering?" In terms of Carr's analysis, let us think of "felt suffering" as the "mental state" of being in pain, or "felt pain," and let us think of the misfortunate circumstances that underlie felt pain as constituting the "unfelt suffering" of the individual who feels pain due to those circumstances. Being malnourished or near starvation might generate felt pain in certain beings whose misfortune it is to be "suffering" those conditions. These beings may also be in a state of sorrow or distress; they would be in a state of sorrow if they recognized (even if they did not feel) the symptoms of their starvation; and they would be in a state of distress even without such recognition. In any of these cases, a compassionate person may "share in their suffering" precisely because she sees the distance between their actual states of diminishment from their possible states of flourishing. This is not a matter of sharing the other's "felt pain" or "inner sensations," whether the other be a human being or some other creature.[10]

What, then, is required for the cat owner to "share in" the cat's suffering and not merely believe *that* the cat "is suffering" a misfortune (similar to what one is vulnerable to)? A clue is provided in one's recognition of one's own suffering. Along with the pain of one's suffering (e.g., sorrow, grief, sadness, woe, diminishment) one wishes relief from it precisely in so far as one realizes that such relief would promote one's own good, one's own flourishing. One's "suffering with" the other, similarly, includes one's experiencing pain (suffering, sorrow, sadness) while also "imaginatively reconstructing" or "engaging" or "sharing" that desire for the relief of suffering (the wish for well-being, the instinct for survival) that one judges appropriate to the circumstances of a particular being suffering a particular misfortune. The qualities of the sufferings one feels are, in a sense, one's own; but the being that one suffers for (and hence "with," assuming that the other "suffers" as well) is the other; and the relief that one seeks is for the other's *suffering*, i.e., for the diminishment caused by the other's situation or circumstances, because of one's wish to promote the good of the *other*. In short, compassion is a "suffering-striving" with another (others). It is in striving to relieve the other's suffering that, as Shantideva puts it, one takes the other's suffering "for one's own." It is the possibility of "striving with" the other that Carr's examples of "unfelt suffering" call into question. Of course one cannot strive with, nor even have pity for, the distant relative whose death never comes to one's attention. Nor is it clear how one can strive with and render aid to someone who is permanently comatose. Instead of Carr's examples, think of these: a stranger or friend is rendered unconscious by (what appears to be) a drug overdose or heart failure or a fall down the stairs. Such victims of unfortunate circumstances are in states of suffering (distress, woe) and, even though they do not experience "felt pain," they may evoke in us genuine compassion.

It is crucial to note the particular contribution that "empathy" plays in enabling one to act compassionately. Consider this case offered by Smith.

> What are the pangs of a mother, when she hears the moanings of her infant, that, during the agony of the disease, cannot express what it feels? In her idea of what it suffers, she joins, to its real helplessness, her own consciousness of that helplessness, and her own terrors for the unknown consequences of its disorder; and out of all these, forms for her own sorrow, the most complete image of misery and distress. The infant, however, feels only the uneasiness of the present instant, which can never be great. (Smith, 1969:8)

The mother's consciousness of her infant's suffering extends far beyond, but nevertheless includes, the infant's own feeling of "uneasiness;" and, clearly it is not (just) the infant's present (or future) feelings of uneasiness that the mother is motivated to rescue her infant from. Suppose the mother were a medical doctor and suppose that upon visiting her best childhood friend whom she has not seen in years, she encounters her friend's infant with a disease very similar to that which afflicted her own child. While she might be able to provide some relief of the uneasiness currently experienced by her friend's child, she might also, being empathetic with the sufferings both of the child and her mother, decide to extend her stay and to utilize her medical training and other personal resources to maximize the chances of saving the life of the child. The painful experience with her own diseased child perhaps makes an empathetic identification in such a situation more likely; and, in turn, her taking on the sufferings of others as though they were her own, underlies her extensive and selfless efforts to save or protect a child's life, not merely to relieve felt states of uneasiness. As Smith acutely notes, "Sympathy, therefore, does not arise so much from the passion, as from the situation which excites it." (Smith, 1969:7)

Indeed, one might well wonder whether there is any "feeling" involved with "sympathy" *per se*. "Empathy" denotes one's *general* capacity to "see" or "feel" what another is experiencing or might (come to) experience, and, so, is broadly associated with "fellow feeling." Often, one's empathy accounts for one's being attuned to or sharing in another's suffering; but notice, this need not lead to one's being "sympathetic" at all. A sadistic or malicious person might well determine what another's vulnerabilities are and then cause that person to suffer acutely; in such a case, the agent might take delight in being attuned to or sharing in another's suffering and so not be motivated to alleviate the other's suffering. By contrast the sympathetic person takes merciful concern for beings who suffer and seeks to alleviate their sufferings. What is clear, in the case of the sadistic or malicious person and in the case of the sympathetic person, is that what motivates behavior is not the empathetic sharing of another's suffering, but the "attitude" that one takes in response to one's awareness of another's suffering.

Compassion, we may conclude, is a "suffering with" other beings that engenders sufficient concern for those beings' overall good to motivate one to perform helpful actions. I think that this articulates the "primitive response" that Charles Taylor identifies as "compassion" and which was clearly and courageously evidenced in the deeds of Samuel and Pearl Oliner. One is compassionate to the extent that one "suffers with" others, is *thereby* concerned for the overall good of (those) others, and *therefore* is motivated to perform (appropriate) helpful actions for their sake. Compassionate response is not to another's "pain" *per se* but to the being who suffers unnecessarily. Often some pain is necessary for one's own good, for one's development; obviously, to shelter a child from all pain would not show appropriate concern for a child's growth, maturity, and autonomy. This is why it is incorrect to define "compassionate acts" simply as "acts that alleviate suffering and pain."[11]

As understood in the Buddhist tradition, compassion is an emotional responsiveness to suffering generally. According to the Dalai Lama, "compassion is the wish that all sentient beings be free of suffering" (Dalai Lama, 2001:96); but this presumes that this wish is fervent, operative, for, as he clarifies, "True compassion has the intensity and spontaneity of a loving mother caring for her suffering baby." (Dalai Lama, 2001:105) The Dalai Lama elaborates on the nature of compassion as follows:

> When I speak of basic human feeling . . . I refer to the capacity we all have to empathize with one another, which in Tibetan we call *shen dug ngal wa la mi sö pa*. Translated literally this means "the inability to bear the sight of another's suffering." Given that this is what enables us to enter into and to some extent participate in others' pain, it is one of our most significant characteristics. It is what causes us . . . to recoil at the sight of harm done to another, to suffer when confronted with others' suffering. (Dalai Lama, 1999:64)

Given the distinction just drawn between "empathy" and "sympathy," I think it is clear that the Dalai Lama's concept of "compassion" is the uniting of the two. The genuinely compassionate person does not merely believe that one should act or wish that one might act; the compassionate person both suffers and strives with suffering beings. This view is reflected in the analyses of both Schopenhauer and Scheler. Interestingly, it also echoes what Augustine and Thomas Aquinas have to say about mercy: "As Augustine says . . . *mercy is heartfelt sympathy for another's distress, impelling us to succor him if we can.* For mercy takes its name *misericordia* from denoting a man's compassionate heart (*miserum cor*), at the sight of another's unhappiness [distress]." (Aquinas, *ST*, II-II, Q. 30, Art. 1)[12]

Finally, it is important also to clearly differentiate compassion from other altruistic attitudes. One who is void of compassion for another cannot perform compassionate acts for that being, since, being void of compassion, one does not truly suffer with the other and *therefore* act for the good of the other. In this respect compassion is clearly different from "mercy" or "kindness," as we ordinarily employ these terms. One can imagine the most self-centered and ruthless monarch showing mercy "on a whim" to a villainous criminal (or, say, in hopes of seducing the criminal's daughter). Similarly, one may engage in a random act of kindness either out of some fleeting inclination or from a self-interested motive completely divorced from "the good" of the recipient of the kindness. Unlike some forms of altruistic conduct, compassionate acts necessarily express an altruistic emotional attitude.

Open-hearted responsiveness to suffering is compassion. Compassion, thus understood, is inherently "impartial" and, hence, distinct from "care." Certainly, the opportunities for "doing good" generally arise when we are dealing with those individuals with whom we are in close contact, e.g., one's family members, one's fellow workers or clients, one's friends and neighbors, and so on; and, clearly, the "householder" has responsibilities for one's family and community which the renunciate does not have. The caveat is that one's caring for one's significant others should not be at the cost of causing intentional suffering to any (human) being to which one stands in a less significant relationship or in no special relationship at all. A mother's sacrifice for *her child* indeed is naturally spontaneous, unmediated by ideas, precepts, or ulterior motives; so, too, in passing beyond the barrier of one's "ego," (one's) innate compassion naturally and spontaneously embraces the sufferings and strivings of other living beings. At first, it might appear paradoxical to suggest that to suffer/strive with other beings in their uniqueness is to treat them impartially. But it works this way: I act partially when I act out of my particular relations with others—for instance, when I treat another as my child, my student, my friend, my neighbor, and so on—*and* when I treat my non-children, non-students, non-friends, etc. contrawise. But why should I not treat my non-children as I would my own or, even, how their parents would treat them, or how their parents would have me treat them? Perhaps to know what is best for the child, I need to see her from the point of view that I would have as the child's parent or that her parent would have or that a best-friend or neighbor would have. My responsibility is to act towards any being with the same degree of concern as I would act toward the being for whom I care most. To take up this responsibility is to adopt a genuinely moral orientation to the world of living

beings it is to be, like Samuel Oliner, a good Samaritan, a righteous one, a bodhisattva.

NOTES

1. Brian Carr reflects, "And of course the man who pities is moved in normal circumstances to aid the one who is suffering—though this was overlooked by Aristotle" (Carr,
1996:418). Carr does note that Aristotle did not consider pity to be a virtue, but errs in thinking that Aristotle intended to analyze all emotions according to their "affective, cognitive and
motivational components," and, in the case of pity, simply failed to mention the third, i.e., the
altruistic concern to help the object of one's pity.

2. Nussbaum offers a sophisticated analysis of compassion in *Upheavals of Thought: The
Intelligence of Emotions* (2001). There she continues to attribute to Aristotle the view that
compassion consists of three cognitive elements: (a) the belief that the person's suffering is
serious; (b) the belief that the person does not deserve the suffering; and (c) the belief that
one's possibilities are similar to those of the sufferer. (2001:306; cf. 1996: 31f) However, she
goes well beyond Aristotle to broaden considerably the meaning of (c) to include similarities
in "vulnerabilities." (2001:315-16) So, even if I do not share the possibility of ever being in
the situation that the one suffering is in, say that I am a male member of the majority class and
the other is a woman of a minority class that suffers from unwarranted exclusions or that the
other is an animal suffering fright from circumstances that I could never face, I might still
realize my own vulnerabilities to being unjustifiably excluded or severely frightened and,
hence, be able to share in the other's suffering. Her analysis then becomes doubly removed
from Aristotle's when she points out that even the more broadly configured (c) is not necessary for compassion; rather, what is necessary, says Nussbaum, is (c*) the *eudaimonistic*
judgment that the one who is suffering (or, as I would prefer, the *relieving* of the other's suffering) is an important part of one's own "scheme of goals and projects;" and it is for the for-
mation of (c*) that (c) is often indispensable. (2001:321-24) Nussbaum then argues convinc-
ingly that (a)-(c*) entails altruistic motivation, while denying that *eudaimonistic* judgments are
necessarily egoistic. (2001:335-40)

I find Nussbaum's account to be insightful and cogent. What I find difficult to accept is
her continued insistence that the notion of compassion that she sketches is at the heart of a
continuous story that moves from Homeric poetry through Aristotle, the ancient Stoics, the
philosophers of the Enlightenment and into contemporary discussions of social theory and
experimental psychology. Indeed, we have seen how her analysis goes well beyond Aristotle's
text on pity. Nussbaum interestingly acknowledges (2001:324) that the bodhisattva, who has
severed himself from vulnerability to pain, and, hence, from the fear of suffering himself, or
even (we might add) of seeing a loved one suffer, may yet have compassion. Clearly, this is
not Aristotle's pitier. But when Nussbaum discusses the Stoic's rejection of compassion—on
the bases of falsity in judgment, impartiality, and its connection with anger (e.g., at the source
of undeserved suffering)—she has Aristotle very much in mind rather than the broader view
she favors that includes the bodhisattva. (2001:356-64) Similarly, she takes Nietzsche to be an
enemy of compassion, whereas he was a critic of "pity" classically understood and not of
"compassion," at least as Schopenhauer understood it. See note #3 below.

3. As David Cartwright (1988) has brilliantly demonstrated, Schopenhauer's *Mitlied*
("Compassion") simply is not Nietzsche's *Mitlied* ("Pity"). Scheler (also uncovers Nietzsche's
"completely *misguided evaluation* of fellow-feeling, and especially of pity." (1954:17) See
also Carr (1996) as well as Blum (1980a).

4. The following is taken from *A Treatise of Human Nature*, Bk. II-II, Sections VII-IX (Hume, 1978:368-399).

5. That "emotional identification" normally is not characteristic of fellow-feeling generally, and hence not of compassion, is a point belabored by Scheler (1954, Ch 2). In commenting on the Confucian notion of the Golden Rule (*shu*), Fingarette observes:

> Yet *shu* does not go so far as to lead me to abandon my own judgment and to become the other person. The task, in *shu*, is twofold. The first step . . . is to imagine what it is to be the other person in the situation in question; the second step, however, is to ask what I, Fingarette, would want, being the person in that situation. For in the last analysis, *shu* calls on me to do as I would want to be done by. (Fingarette, 1979:385)

I think that the Buddhist view of the Golden Rule would amend this analysis in one important respect. It is not simply how I would want to be treated that is determinative of how I should treat another, but it is how I would best judge that I might be benefited that is determinative. What one should not lose sight of is *one's own understanding* of how the person who is suffering might be benefited. This point is illustrated in an example that Fingarette (1979:387) subsequently provides.

6. Remarking on a film documentary on righteous gentiles [Pierre Sauvage's *Weapons of the Spirit: A Documentary*, 1989], James Fodor perceptively observes, "several of the peasants, mostly women, responded to the question, "Why did you help these Jewish refugees?," with something as simple and opaque as: 'It's the human thing to do. That's all.' Or, 'it was the normal thing to do'; 'it happened quite naturally,' or 'it happened by itself.'" (Fodor, 2002:413, n19) Such responses are typical and reflect the fact that "everyday" compassion (often) is "a primitive response" that involves an "immediate" participation in another's suffering; and this means that there are no more basic structures (e.g., Hume's "pain" + "benevolence" or Smith's "imaginative projection") in terms of which it needs to be analyzed.

7. Given Blum's formal analysis of compassion, it is perhaps curious that he should observe: "Compassion seems restricted to beings capable of feeling or being harmed. Bypassing the question of compassion for plants, animals, institutions, I will focus on persons as objects of compassion. (1980b:507) While it is natural for philosophers to focus on compassion for persons, an analysis of a concept should account for the full range of its (non-borderline) applications. In particular, an analysis of "compassion" should take into account its clear application to animals since it is commonly understood that animals can "suffer" and that compassionate persons can and do share in their suffering. Even if Blum's basic account is amended to cover sentient beings as appropriate objects of compassion, it remains defective for three reasons. First, it *might* seem that one's "compassion" could encompass only one other or only a few other beings. Often Blum's examples of acts of compassion are situated within family relationships or friendships. Both Blum's examples and his characterization of compassion tend to conflate "compassion" with "caring." Secondly, while "imaginative dwellings" ("reconstructions") or "construals" often do enable one to "participate in" another's situation and, hence, "to suffer with" the other, what if such "suffering with" does not result? It would seem that Blum's conditions could be fulfilled by one's merely having an "empathetic" concern for another's suffering "of a certain degree of intensity" but not sufficient to motivate (and sustain) altruistic conduct; this falls short, it seems to me, of what the emotional attitude of compassion signifies. Imaginative dwellings, then, are neither necessary nor sufficient to generate "suffering with" another. And, thirdly, Blum's analysis presents a series of characteristics but does not explain how they are interrelated, of one piece.

8. Fellow-feeling, for Scheler, is a noteworthy capacity of human beings precisely because it signifies direct communion with others and, hence, refutes the Cartesian view of the "privacy" of an individual's experience and the necessity of analogical reasoning or inference (based on one's own experience) in one's forming some idea of what emotions another being experiences. Scheler clearly anticipates Wittgenstein on the very critical point that mental state concepts embrace both "inner states" and "observable behavior."

the other person has—like ourselves—a sphere of absolute personal privacy, which can never be given to us. But that 'experiences' occur there is given for us *in* expressive phenomena—again, not by inference, but directly, as a sort of primary 'perception'. It is *in* the blush that we perceive shame, *in* the laughter joy. . . . For the relationship here referred to is a *symbolic*, not a causal one. (Scheler, 1954:10)

9. See Snow, 1993:61. In her earlier article, "Compassion" (1991), Snow follows Lawrence Blum by defining compassion as "a 'suffering with' another that includes an altruistic concern for the other's good" and that beliefs facilitate "benevolent desires for the other's good" in those who *feel* compassion. (Snow, 1991:196-97) So, Snow appears to progress towards a "belief account" of compassion while Nussbaum (2001) came to recognize that her earlier "belief" account was incomplete.

10. Scheler declares:

Christianity brought with it a non-cosmic personal love-mysticism of universal Compassion. It was left to one of the greatest artificers of the spirit in European history to make the memorable attempt of uniting and harnessing this, within a single life stream and the Being of Nature. This was the very remarkable achievement of the saint [Francis] of Assisi. (Scheler, 1954:87)

Since the sixteenth century at least, philosophers have argued that "compassion" or "humaneness" should extend to non-human animals, that is that one should not be cruel to animals and that one should relieve/alleviate their suffering, whenever possible, for their good and not just because of how humans might benefit as a result. Montaigne even wrote of ". . . a general duty to be humane, not only to such animals as possess life and feeling but even to trees and plants" (Passmore, 1975:208); and the extension of "compassion" and "humaneness" to animals was quite prevalent among British philosophers in the eighteenth century. Why not consider plants and institutions as "paradigmatic" sufferers? (See Snow, 1993:66, n12)

11. As does Statman, 1994:339, n25; unfortunately, this leads him to draw the incorrect inference that unwarranted mercy to wrongdoers challenges the view that all compassionate acts are praiseworthy. I discuss this issue in Ch. 3.5.

12. For a recent comparison of the views of Thomas Aquinas and the Dalai Lama, see Barad, 2007. It should be noted however that her account makes no attempt to "reconcile" the Dalai Lama's view that compassion is "impartial" and Aquinas' view that a person ought to love all human beings but not equally, since one should have greater love for those who one is in relationship with than for humanity in general. (Aquinas, *ST* II-II, Q. 26, Art. 6-12) Interestingly, too, the Buddhist-Schopenhauer notion of "compassion" (as well as the Augustine-Aquinas notion of "mercy") may be comparable to Kant's notion of "sympathy." See Ch. III, endnote #11.

Chapter III
Compassion as the Basis of Moral Value

good is to be done and ensued, and evil is to be avoided.

Thomas Aquinas, *Summa Theologica*

The good is what preserves and advances life; evil is what hinders or destroys it. We are ethical . . . if we surrender our strangeness toward other creatures and share in the life and the suffering that surround us. . . . Only then do we possess an inalienable, continuously developing, and self-orienting ethic of our own.

Albert Schweitzer, "Reverence for Life"

The primary task of this chapter is to elucidate the meaning and significance of the two foundational principles of acting compassionately: "One ought not to cause any living being to suffer unnecessarily;" and, "One ought to protect/relieve other living beings from unnecessary suffering." First, I will try to clarify what it means to "act compassionately" and to see oneself under a "moral obligation" to act compassionately. Second, I will present Schopenhauer's case for compassion being the sole source of moral value. Then, I will take up the notion of "justice" and argue that, as *the* cardinal moral virtue, its "demands" are embraced by the principles of compassion. It follows that Kant's distinction between "imperfect duties" and "perfect duties," with the corollary that the former trump the latter, is mistaken; I will demonstrate this by taking Kant's "duty of beneficence," thought by him to be an "imperfect" duty, and show how it is on par with what Kant sees as "perfect duties." This analysis helps to explain how compassion is the basis of all moral value. I conclude this chapter with a few remarks on how one might bridge an ethic of compassion with "care" ethics as well as with an ethics of Christian love.

1. "Acting Compassionately" and Being Compassionate

In an instructive article, "Compassion and Commanded Love" (1994), Dana Radcliffe shows how Blum's (1980a) analysis of compassion as involving imaginative reconstruction fits into Robert Roberts' (1984) general analysis of emotions as "serious construals" to yield an affirmative answer to the question of whether "*agapēic* compassion" can be voluntarily developed and, hence, be prescribed or commanded. Radcliffe suggests:

> on the construal theory, one exercises one's voluntary control over compassion in a certain kind of situation by bringing to bear relevant concepts, thoughts, paradigms, and images relating to people's general weal and woe, their common humanity, and specific human needs. One applies these concepts, etc., in one's construal of the other person's situation of need, as one attends to various aspects of his situation and imaginatively reconstructs his experience. By such means, one is sometimes able to summon up compassion which then motivates one to perform helping actions one would not have had sufficient incentive to do. (Radcliffe, 1994:59)

Another way of expressing the form of control exercised here is to say that a certain intensity of compassion (or empathy) that might be sufficient to initiate one's imaginative dwelling on the situation of a suffering person might not be sufficient to motivate helping behavior until one imaginatively dwells on the other's situation so to generate the intensity of compassion necessary to (overcome internal resistance and) motivate the appropriate helping responses.

Radcliffe sees the Gospel's "Love Commandment" as obligating one to not only act lovingly (compassionately) but to be loving (compassionate), that is to act from love (compassion). If compassion is available within one's nature as a human being and can be generated or summoned, then, does it not make sense to think that God might command us to be compassionate (to our "neighbors")? And, if so, then would it not also make sense to think: "One (always) ought to *be* compassionate?" Might not this be the supreme principle of morality?

Being compassionate, spontaneously acting from compassion is a state of moral perfection. As such, it might serve as an aspiration but not as a realizable goal for most agents "here and now." The closest one might come, I think, to a realizable standard of compassion in the here and now of decision-making is to *decide to act* compassionately, to intentionally protect or relieve beings from suffering out of a concern for their well being. But, this might require deliberate or reflective effort.[1]

One is under moral obligation, as it were, when there is a recognized distance between one's self, or at least some of one's tendencies, dispositions or priorities, and what one believes *ought* to be done. This insight provides additional context for Nel Noddings' point that maternal caring is "natural" and not "ethical"—presumably because it springs from natural inclinations—and that we do not credit ethical behavior to maternal animals that take care of their offspring. (1984:79) But, of course, even though we *might* not credit a person who protects her child from maternal instinct or inclination, especially when no great risk or sacrifice on her part is necessary, we certainly would morally blame her if she fails to do so. One explanation for this is that one should try to live up to the ethical principle of one-caring in situations in which one's caring is called for but where providing such caring is not natural or spontaneous.

Most people on *some* occasions show compassion "naturally." This fact underlies both Taylor's claim that compassion is a "primitive responsiveness" that marks human nature and Schopenhauer's claim that compassion is an "everyday" phenomenon. On the other hand, an agent may aim or *aspire* to act compassionately towards others *always*, i.e., whenever there is opportunity to do so. Adopting such an ideal itself expresses considerable intensity of compassion; however, one might have to "work at it" continually to broaden and deepen one's compassionate responsiveness to the sufferings of the world. A reprehensible failure to act compassionately occurs when one intentionally acts with the aim of not protecting or not relieving a living being from serious suffering (when it was possible to do so); the most grievous of these failures often occur when one intentionally *causes* a living being to suffer unnecessarily. For a being aspiring to act compassionately, these failures are breaches of moral responsibility. On the other hand, not to act kindly or lovingly, in ways over and above protecting or relieving beings from serious suffering, constitutes a failure to act meritoriously; from the point of view of "an ethic of compassion" developed below, such behavior does not constitute a violation of moral obligation.

2. The Principles of Acting Compassionately

Commonly, "first principles" of normative ethics are principles that govern choices of actions since it is decisions about conduct that (a) are under the control of one's will and, hence, (b) result in "good" or "evil" for which one is responsible and may be held accountable. In Mahāyāna Buddhism, one encounters as "pure precepts" the injunctions: "Do not create/cause evil" and "Do good" ("Practice virtue").[2] In Western thought, a similar starting point is what Thomas Aquinas called the "first precept" of the natural (moral) law: *"good is to be done and ensued, and evil is to be avoided"* (*ST*:I-II, Q. 94, Art. 2) This appears tautological, yet three questions emerge quickly upon consideration: "What constitutes 'good' and 'evil'?" "Which is more important, to avoid evil or to do good?" And, "How are 'right' and 'wrong' conduct to be conceived?"

Schopenhauer (1995:147ff) offers an illuminating set of answers to these questions in light of what he identifies as the supreme principle of ethics: *Ne-*

minem laede; imo omnes, quantum potes, juva ("Injure no one; on the contrary, help every one as much as you can"). "Injure no one" is the fundamental principle of justice, argues Schopenhauer, and since its meaning is wholly negative it can be practiced simultaneously by all. "Help every one as much as you can" identifies, for Schopenhauer, the virtue of loving-kindness; and while he does not refer to it as a "principle," it seems to be such. For Schopenhauer, justice and loving-kindness are the two cardinal virtues (from which all others can be derived theoretically as well as in practice) and are rooted in compassion as "two clearly separate degrees wherein another's suffering can directly become my motive...." (Schopenhauer, 1995:148)

It is in reference to the principle of justice that Schopenhauer defines the notions of right and wrong conduct: "The concepts *wrong* and *right* are synonymous with doing harm and not doing harm, and to the latter belongs also the warding off of injury." (Schopenhauer, 1995:154) On this view, the *evil* that is to be avoided is "harm" or "injury" (which I shall identify as serious, unnecessary "suffering"); and the *good* to be pursued is the prevention of harm or injury (or suffering). For Schopenhauer, to act wrongly is to treat someone unjustly; but, it seems, to act rightly includes more than the simple negation of this, i.e., not to treat someone unjustly, for it also includes "warding off of injury" which, it would appear, is embraced by the principle of loving-kindness, "Help every one as much as you can."

Schopenhauer understands the import of the fundamental Eastern insight that "evil" is the suffering of injury or harm and "good" is the absence of such suffering.[3] Thus, *moral evil* is the intentionality to cause injury or harm and *moral good* is the intentionality to preserve (protect, relieve) beings from injury of harm. Hence, it always is morally wrong to intentionally cause injury to another, i.e., suffering unnecessary for the other's overall good, and it is sometimes morally wrong to willfully fail to prevent (or provide relief from) such injury, e.g., when one sees correctly that prevention is possible without directly causing unnecessary suffering to another; conversely, one acts rightly by refraining to intentionally cause injury and by doing what one can to prevent injury or to provide relief from injuries incurred.

If we restate Schopenhauer's "supreme principle" in terms of "ought," we get: "One ought not to cause anyone injury (unnecessary suffering)" and "One ought to protect/relieve others from unnecessary suffering" which, in the first-person, may be rationally derived as follows:

1. As a living being, I have a will to live, prosper and avoid unnecessary suffering.
2. All living beings have a will to live, prosper and to avoid unnecessary suffering.
3. I would not wish for any living being to cause me unnecessary suffering.

4. One ought not to treat any living being as one would not wish to be treated.

5. I ought not to cause any living being to suffer unnecessarily.

And:

1a. As a living being, I have a will to live, prosper and avoid unnecessary suffering.

2a. All living beings have a will to live, prosper and avoid unnecessary suffering

3a. I would wish for other living beings to protect/relieve me from unnecessary suffering.

4a. One ought to treat other living beings as one would wish to be treated by them.

5a. I ought to protect/relieve other living beings from unnecessary suffering.

We may call (5) and (5a) "the principles of compassion," the former being a "principle of duty" and the latter being a "principle of aspiration." Together, they may be said to constitute the grounds of "moral responsibility" according to the ethic of compassion. These principles are expressed in the first person for, as Albert Schweitzer's comment states, what is important is for human beings to "possess an inalienable, continuously developing, self-orienting ethic of our own."[4] What these principles mean, how they are interpreted in terms of "precepts" or "mindfulness trainings," reflect one's experiential understanding and integration of them in one's life. As the succeeding chapters make clear, from the point of view of an ethic of compassion, there is no "moral authority" over and above the individual; indeed, to seek to impose values on others, rather than to encourage others to cultivate compassion as their own moral orientation, is itself not to treat persons compassionately.

Some comment on premises (1)-(4) is in order. Premises (1) and (2) echo in reverse Aristotle's dictum that "All human beings desire to be happy," from which one surmises, "Since I am a human being, I desire to be happy." The main difference, of course, is that (2) ranges over all "living beings" rather than the narrower class of "human beings." By a "living being," I mean a "sentient being" and to exclude "vegetative" beings or plants. Following the Buddhist tradition, Damien Keown views a "living being" as an ontologically distinct ensemble of five constituent elements: (a) bodily *form*, (b) *feeling* or capacity to respond effectively to stimuli; (c) *character* in the sense of a pattern of dispositions or habits or tendencies; (4) *spirit* or "sentiency" (sometimes referred to as "consciousness"); and (5) *karma* or a moral history. (Keown, 1995b:23-26) Accordingly, so-called "higher animals" are regarded as "living beings;" even insects are so regarded, but plants and microorganisms are not. Fortunately, given our purposes, we need not define precisely the extension of this concept for, as will be noted, the principles and precepts of acting compassionately are applied to what one "knows" or "takes" to be a living being. We may even disregard for now the element of *karma*, since it does not constitute an *independent* criterion of a "living being" over and above the possession of the remaining four characteristics.[5]

The notion of "unnecessary suffering" employed above is meant to do double duty. It denotes suffering that is both "avoidable" and "not required" for the overall benefit of the being who suffers. Furthermore, these features are self-regarding as well as other-regarding. Premise (1)-(1a) states that as a living being I will to avoid unnecessary suffering which implies, I think, that I will to protect myself from unnecessary suffering. From this, two corollaries follow. Failure to protect oneself from unnecessary suffering is done in ignorance or not willfully. The ethic of compassion, in so far as it sets standards for rational self-governance, is not a purely altruistic, other-regarding ethic; one should treat oneself as well as others compassionately.

Premise (1)-(1a) incorporates the awareness of one's own suffering, of the numerous ways in which one is vulnerable to suffering. At the root of one's vulnerability is the very nature of "life" or "living being." "Death," "old age," "disease" or "illness," "pain," "want," "disappointment," and so on constitute (part of) the fabric of "life." One's own experiences as well as one's reason and imagination regarding one's vulnerabilities enable one to recognize the extent of an individual's own suffering or potential to suffer. Premise (2) then carries this awareness over to all living beings; for the general vulnerabilities to suffering that I have are shared by all other beings, who, like me, are "living." In short, what one sees is that "they are me." This way of thinking is the opposite of what "pity" implies. As we have seen, pity results from the recognition, first, of others' sufferings and, second, the recognition that I am similarly situated or vulnerable, to, third, the recognition that "I could be (in the future) them."

The proffered "rationality" of the principles of compassion clearly relies on the Golden Rule in step (4) and (4a). When the Golden Rule is combined with premises (1)-(3) or (1a)-(3a), then it is not simply "how one would wish to be treated" that establishes the ground of acting towards others (or even towards oneself), but rather it is "one's will to avoid unnecessary suffering" that establishes this ground. Paraphrasing Schopenhauer (1995:165-66) to suffer with another is not to feel "our pain" in his shoes, but to share in *his* suffering. What might remedy the pain *we* would feel in another's shoes might not remedy the pain *he* is feeling; and, more importantly, it might not alleviate the other's suffering.

The concluding statements (5) and (5a) are The Principles of Acting Compassionately: avoid doing evil, i.e., avoid causing unnecessary suffering; and, do good, i.e., protect or relieve beings from unnecessary suffering. In Chapter IV, we will see how (5) underlies negative "rules" of moral obligation, akin to "One ought not to kill/steal/lie/commit adultery/etc. Chapter V considers how (5a) underlies positive "rules" of moral conduct such as "One ought to respect life, be kind, speak honestly, honor one's commitments, and so on. As mentioned above, the second principle is subordinated to the first, one should not benefit some being(s) by intentionally harming other beings.

3. Justice, the Cardinal Moral Virtue

The root meaning of "justice"—as presumed in the discussion of received views in Book I of Plato's *Republic* and echoed in Augustine (*On Free Choice of the Will*, I.13)—is to give each person his or her due; injustice, then, is to deprive a person of his or her due. Often, what one is due or what one is owed depends on the nature of one's relationship with the other. If the relationship between two agents is a contractual one, then it would appear that justice lies in fulfilling the terms of the contract. However, Plato's Socrates in Book I of *The Republic* points out that on the assumption that "as between friends, what one owes to another is to do him good, not harm" it follows that "to repay money entrusted to one is not to render what is due, if the two parties are friends and the repayment proves harmful to the lender."[6] What one owes someone *qua* friend may override what one owes that individual *qua* lender. A contractarian here might say that when two persons become friends they each voluntarily assume a responsibility to promote the well being of the other and this provides grounds for one party to the friendship to make a claim on the other for beneficence. But what if the other is a stranger? What of the severely wounded soldier encountered by Samuel Oliner? What of the battered traveler that both the Levite and the Samaritan encounter as discussed by Jesus? (*Luke*, 10:30-36) Does one owe another, a stranger, *qua* human being anything?

Joel Feinberg has pointed out, "In our time it is commonplace to speak of *needs* as "constituting claims" and that the cry of one in serious need is a "claim against the world." (Feinberg, 1980:140) The notion that obligations are correlative to *claims* rather than to *rights* was emphasized by William James: "...the moment we take a steady look at the question, *we see not only that without a claim actually made by some concrete person there can be no obligation, but that there is some obligation wherever there is a claim.* Claim and obligation are, in fact, coextensive terms; they cover each other exactly." (James, 1968: 617) In a similar vein, W.D. Ross suggests that my *prima facie* duties, including the duty of "not injuring others" as well as "duties of beneficence," are grounded on *claims on me*. Says Ross, "It would be quite natural to say, 'a person to whom I have made a promise has a claim on me', and also, 'a person whose distress I could relieve (at the cost of breaking the promise) has a claim on me'." (Ross, 1988:20)

That others' suffering grounds the notions of justice and moral responsibility is central to the work of Simone Weil and Emmanuel Levinas. Writes Weil: "Justice consists in seeing that no harm is done to men. Whenever a man cries inwardly: 'Why am I being hurt?' harm is being done to him. He is often mis-

taken when he tries to define the harm, and why and by whom it is being inflicted on him. But the cry itself is infallible." (Weil, 1977:334) Levinas refers
to the cry of suffering as an "appeal" and he observes, "since the Other looks at
me, I am responsible for him, without having *taken* on responsibilities in his
regard; his responsibility *is incumbent on me*." (Levinas, 1985:96)

I think this notion of being responsible for another is similar to the Buddhist
notion of being responsive to the other as articulated in Shantideva's *The Way of
the Bodhisattva*, 8:95:

> Since I and other beings both,
> In fleeing suffering, are equal and alike,
> What difference is there to distinguish us,
> That I should strive to save myself and not the other? (1997:123)

Furthermore, this "impartiality" of self and other should extend to all others and
among all others.[7] Yet, clearly we often are unable to help relieve the sufferings
of all the beings we encounter, let alone which exist. Suppose that Paul Oliner
and the Good Samaritan had encountered three individuals in need of dire assistance but that the time and resources at hand allowed for life-saving aid to be
given to only one. While one cannot be obligated or expected to do the impossible, it does not take much effort (especially for ethicists) to imagine all kinds of
scenarios that give rise to issues of fairness regarding the distribution of available aid resources. Should a principle of *distributive* justice govern one's compassionate responsiveness to others?

Aristotle pointedly acknowledges (*Nic. Eth.*, Bk.5) a "general" sense of
justice as denoting the whole of virtue, although he is more concerned with "particular justice" that focuses on fairness in distribution. These two senses of "justice" are prominent in the *Oxford English Dictionary*'s account of current usage.
"Distributive justice" or "fairness" as the cardinal *social* (political) virtue is
what philosophers like John Rawls are exclusively concerned with. (Rawls,
1971:7ff) In order for fairness to be an issue for an agent, one must be empow-
ered to distribute benefits (or punishments) for the common good of others in
light of one's social roles or relationships within the context of institutional values that promote the common good. Socially engaged citizens do well to assure
that social policies relieve injustices to the greatest possible extent.

For Schopenhauer, on the other hand, it is the general sense of an *individual's* refraining from injustice that is identified with "giving others their due."
He puts the matter this way: "Contrary to appearance, the negative meaning of
justice is established even in the trite definition, 'Give to each his own.' If a man
has his own, there is no need to give it to him; and so the meaning is, 'Take from
no one what is his own.'" (Schopenhauer, 1995:153) As we have seen, however,
those who suffer grievously, *qua* human (sentient) beings, have a legitimate
claim "against the world" to the alleviation of their sufferings. So, I think it better to say that to give others their due requires that we not only refrain from injustice but also that we not willfully fail to help relieve others of unnecessary,

grievous suffering. It follows then, that precepts proscribing (types of actions that typically result in) the doing of evil and precepts prescribing the doing of good are both ways of justice; one is just, gives others their due, by not acting unjustly towards them and, if they suffer seriously, one is just in doing good by them. There is no moral constraint on how compassionate responsiveness to others is to be "distributed" as long as one acts with the intention of doing good by relieving impartially the sufferings of others ("as if they were one's own").[8]

4. Does Morality Have a Unified Nature?

In *Friendship, Altruism, and Morality* (1980b), Lawrence Blum develops several insightful lines of argument to show how the Kantian ethical framework can neither defeat nor accommodate the moral value of altruism. *Contra* Kant, Blum makes the case (Ch. 2) that altruistic emotions have the constancy, impartiality, strength and availability required to guide conduct of moral value. On the other hand, Blum rejects any attempt to ground all moral value on compassion or the altruistic attitudes more generally. In short, morality has no "unified nature." (Blum 1980b:8-9)

> And so altruistic emotions need not be grounded in moral principles in order for us to act on them freely and spontaneously in situations in which no moral demands are made on us, while yet not acting on them freely and spontaneously in situations in which moral demands are made on us (and in which acting from altruistic emotions would or might fail to honor the demands). (Blum, 1980b:107; cf. 163-67)

But if there is no "unified moral nature," how can Blum be so confident in adopting a Kantian view in holding that "moral demands" *always* trump (incompatible) altruistic concerns? Conversely, if our moral nature is bifurcated, how might one *rationally* determine that, in some situations, acting "altruistically" has moral value and, even, more such value than fulfilling a conflicting demand of "duty?"

In *The Metaphysics of Morals*, Part II, Kant distinguishes between "perfect" and "narrow" ethical duties on the one hand and "imperfect" and "wide" ethical duties on the other. Examples of the former are the duties not to lie, to keep one's promises, and to repay one's debts; examples of the latter are duties to develop one's talents, duties of gratitude and friendship, and duties to help others in need and to perfect oneself morally. Perfect/narrow duties are wholly determinate: it is clear precisely what is to be done, when, how, and for whom; failure to fulfill duties merits contempt, moral censure. Imperfect/wide duties do not specify morally required behavior on any given occasion, as in the case of "duties of love" which include duties of beneficence, gratitude and sympathy. It is up to the agent to embody or to express such virtues, but how this is carried out is a matter of discretion. Failure to act beneficently on any given occasion does not merit moral contempt since it does not inherently constitute a transgression of duty. On the other hand, for Kant, one is never justified in willingly failing to fulfill a perfect duty; hence, acting "beneficently" in lieu of fulfilling a determinate obligation to another is never morally worthy.[9]

A Kantian theorist might hold that acts of compassion, such as the Good Samaritan's, are not required acts of moral obligation or duty since the recipients can claim no "right" against the specific individual(s) rendering aid. Furthermore, the Kantian might wonder, if any particular act of compassion lies outside the scope of what is morally required, then how can such an act be morally justified when its performance necessitates a transgression of a perfect moral duty (to respect someone's "rights"), if all intentional transgressions of such duties are blameworthy? We might say, then, that willful failure to fulfill a perfect duty constitutes a violation of a Kantian principle of morality, e.g., fails to respect humanity as an end in itself or fails to instantiate a maxim which can be willed as a universal law.[10] What I now aim to show is how we may disengage the notion of a "*moral* duty of justice" from Kant's notion of a "perfect duty." It then will make sense to *ask*, "Might not a duty of 'beneficence' be a duty of 'justice' so that sometimes failures to fulfill duties of beneficence constitute serious acts of injustice and that sometimes acting beneficently is morally required?"

Kant claims: "To be beneficent, that is, to promote according to one's means the happiness of others in need, without hoping of something in return, is everyone's duty." (Kant, 1996c:572) A duty of beneficence follows from Kant's supreme principle, the Categorical Imperative, since, on Kant's view, it is impossible for one to will universally a maxim of not helping others, for such a will would conflict with itself since often situations arise in which he would need (hence will) the assistance of others.[11] In *Lectures on Ethics*, Kant makes a three-fold distinction:

> Acts which have in view the welfare of another and are prompted by and proportioned to his wants are acts of kindness. They may be magnanimous, if they entail the sacrifice of an advantage; they are acts of benevolence if they alleviate real needs; and if they alleviate the extreme necessities of life they are acts of charity. (Kant, 1979:235)

Following Schopenhauer, "acts of compassion" would comprise Kantian acts of benevolence and (especially) charity; whereas Kantian acts of kindness, are proportioned to the recipient's "wants"—not "needs"—and, if undone, would not promote or ignore another's (serious) suffering. Accordingly, let us employ the notion, "duty of beneficence*," to refer to one's duty to perform "benevolent" and "charitable" acts as identified by Kant. That one has a duty of beneficence* does not mean, of course, that one has a duty to act from a "benevolent" motive or from a "sympathetic" feeling. While one might have particular sympathy for the plight of a family member, a friend or a neighbor, one should be beneficent to whomever is in need—whether one has a particular feeling for that person or not. Of course, to say that one has a duty to be beneficent to "whomever is in need" should not be thought to imply that one has a duty to "all" (or "each") who are in need; for, "ought implies can" and one cannot possibly help everyone in need. Rather, if one encounters another in (dire) need, then one is at least "called" upon to offer that person aid, whomever it might be. The other's suffering, as we have seen, makes *a claim of justice* on the passerby. We might say of the Good Samaritan, then, that she has a duty of beneficence* *specifically* to aid the battered traveler at hand, assuming that she is not thereby (intentionally) causing serious suffering upon another, and even should she knowingly forego fulfilling a promise or some "perfect duty." Such a specific "duty of beneficence" is a "moral duty of justice" in that it renders what is "due" to a person by virtue of that person's humanity; in failing to provide assistance, one disrespects the humanity of the victim.

Reasoning from the Golden Rule, the Good Samaritan may think, "I would wish/accept another's breaking a routine promise to me to help someone in dire need, and, so I will treat my friend in this circumstance as I would wish/accept being treated." It might even be argued that a maxim of the sort, "I shall keep all promises except in circumstances when not doing so does not cause significant harm and is urgently necessary to the well-being of another," can be willed to be a universal law. Acting compassionately can, in standard case-scenarios, be accommodated by one's sense of what one ought and ought not to do on the basis of a universal principle. We might say that if our Good Samaritan acts from a maxim in light of the Golden Rule, then she acts dutifully and compassionately, although not *from* compassion or what Blum calls "direct altruism." Or, if one so acts from compassion, then her act has moral value and accords with what she ought to do or is morally justified in doing, although she then is not acting *from* duty. What confers "moral value" on *conduct* is not the *motive* from which one acts, e.g., whether it is the motive of benevolence or the motive of duty, but the *intention* with which one acts. The compassionate person, as illustrated by Samuel Oliner, may act spontaneously, without deliberation or reflection or concern for moral principles. He does not act out of a principled belief as to what he ought to do; he does not act from a sense of moral duty or from respect for the moral law. For Blum, such "direct altruism" is a source of moral value since one is motivated by a concern for the good of another. Suppose a Kantian agent were in a situation identical to Oliner's and, out of "the duty of beneficence," acted as Oliner did. Let us say that the Kantian agent was motivated out of a deliberated sense of moral duty but that Oliner was motivated from altruism. Why should one agent's *act* have more moral value than the other? Both agents intentionally acted compassionately, that is, acted with the intention of relieving suffering ("as if it were one's own").[12]

In summary, we saw that compassion is the capacity to "suffer and strive with" another; to share in another being's suffering and to strive (with that being) to alleviate its suffering. Although the capacity for compassion is a "primitive" constituent of human nature, often other aspects of one's individuality tend to frustrate or block our acting compassionately when situations calling for compassion arise. This gives rise to the notion of "an ethics of compassion," the sense that one ought to act compassionately in a deliberative, reflective, principled manner if not "spontaneously." From this point of departure, I argued that it makes sense for a moral agent to commit herself or himself to two principles of acting compassionately: "I ought not to cause any living being to suffer unnecessarily" and "I ought to protect/relieve other living beings from unnecessary suffering." If morality bids one "to do good" and "to avoid doing evil," if, that is to say, the "moral value" of conduct resides in its promoting "well-being" and minimizing "suffering," then the "intentionality" of so acting is the locus of our moral nature; whether this be expressed "directly" or "deliberatively" reflects perhaps a difference in moral development, but not a difference in the moral value of one's conduct.

5. Appendix: Love and Justice in the Gospels

Certainly, people identifying themselves as "Christian" often live a life that accords with the ethics of compassion. Francis of Assisi, Albert Schweitzer and Mother Teresa were exemplary practitioners; and there have been countless others. In the (Orthodox) Christian tradition, it is in "purity of heart" that one achieves total openness or selflessness. Saint Isaac of Syria says of "purity of heart:"

> It is a heart filled with compassion for the whole of created nature...And what is a compassionate heart? It is a heart which burns for all creation, for the birds, for the beasts, for the devils, for every creature. When he thinks about them, when he looks at them, his eyes fill with tears. So strong, so violent is his compassion . . . that his heart breaks when he sees the pain and suffering of the humblest creature. (Forest, 1999:99)

Jesus preached a gospel of love and we have seen in Chapter I that it is love of God and neighbor that underpins the Christian understanding of the Golden Rule. Dana Radcliffe speaks of Jesus as commanding our "love of neighbor," and "neighbor" is taken to mean whomever one is in contact with, friend or foe, acquaintance or stranger, saint or sinner. Indeed, often Jesus emphasizes that one's attention should be directed to the poorest, the neediest among us— relieving their suffering is what it means to seek "justice."

One of the few places where Jesus is commonly understood to be addressing issues of "justice" is in the parable of "The Laborers in the Vineyard."

> For the kingdom of heaven is like a householder who went out early in the morning to hire laborers for his vineyard. After agreeing with the laborers for a denarius a day, he sent them into his vineyard. And going out about the third hour he saw others standing idle in the market place; and to them he said, 'You

go into the vineyard too, and whatsoever is right I will give you.' So they went. Going out again about the sixth and ninth hour, and did the same. And about the eleventh hour he went out and found others standing; and he said to them, 'Why do you stand here idle all day?' They said to him, 'Because no man has hired us.' He said to them, 'Go you into the vineyard too [and whatsoever is right, that shall you receive]' And when evening came, the owner of the vineyard said to his steward, 'Call the laborers and pay them their wages, beginning with the last, up to the first.' And when those hired about the eleventh hour came, each of them received a denarius. Now when the first came, they thought they would receive more; but each of them also received a denarius. And on receiving it they grumbled at the householder, saying, 'These last worked only one hour, and you have made them equal to us who have borne the burden of the day and the scorching heat.' But he replied to one of them, 'Friend, I am doing you no wrong; did you not agree with me for a denarius? Take what belongs to you, and go; I choose to give to this last as I give to you. Am I not allowed to do what I choose with what belongs to me? Or do you begrudge my generosity?' So the last will be first, and the first last. (*Matthew* 20:1-16)

Now, under the standard Aristotelian model of comparative justice (fairness), it appears that something is amiss. For if one is compensating a person *qua* laborer, and if one person provides double or triple the labor of another, then, it might be thought, this is a relevant dissimilarity of effort or production which should lead to a proportionally dissimilar compensation. What Jesus says is that if the first laborers hired are paid their due (what was agreed upon), what right do they have to complain about how others are paid? Theologically, of course, the point of the parable is that while God had promised salvation to his chosen people, and many of these have for years (or even generations) acted righteously and piously, then who is to say that it is unjust for the newly converted to reap the same reward?

A related theological point seems to be this: as God is the master of all, who should dispute what He does with what is His? Nevertheless, God enters into covenants or agreements with man, and the fulfillment of agreements readily accords with man's sense of "justice." Yet, clearly, God is not motivated to do what is right or just *because* it accords with man's sense of justice, e.g., fulfilling a promise; presumably, God acts as He does in recognition of man's deepest needs. Herein lies a profound truth regarding the relationship between compassion and justice. One who acts in responsiveness to another's deepest needs, acts compassionately; and if such action is particularly "undeserved" in a relative or comparative sense, then the act is "merciful" as well. While it might be love that motivates acts of compassion, what love motivates might be just, that is, *justifiable (justified)* upon analysis. One level of justification might be that an act is the fulfillment of a promise; a deeper justification might be that the act redresses another's vulnerability to suffering. Justification, giving justifying reasons, generally is embedded in a second-person or a third-person analysis; it is how one *explains* to *another* (usually, but it is possible to offer such explanations to oneself, say as reminders of) why some conduct was appropriate, has moral value.

As emphasized in Section 1, "acts of compassion" are motivated directly out of altruistic concern or love; "acting compassionately" may be one's response to understanding the act's justification. Compassion as an agent's inner motivation for acting and justice as that act's external rationale are two measures of the same act—the first indicates the good being intended by the agent and the second indicates the good being bestowed upon the recipient.

Let us now take up the question of whether there is a conception of justice being exemplified by the householder in the parable that might serve as a model for just conduct on the part of one person towards others.[13] *Qua* laborer, perhaps the more productive or the more hard-working or the more senior, and so on, should be treated preferentially. But can the same be said of treating persons *qua* persons? Notice that we can analyze the parable from the perspective of non-comparative justice. If a *denarius* is, as there is some evidence for, the daily subsistence wage, and if everyone should be provided his/her daily bread, then everyone is due subsistence or the wage that subsistence requires. The explanation for the householder's claim to the laborers hired late that, "whatsoever is right, that shall ye receive," is that it is right (or just) to give persons *qua* persons what they are due: non-suffering subsistence. We might say, then, that what appears to be "merciful" on the part of the householder in providing the laborers hired late a payment equal to those hired much earlier in the day, is nonetheless "just" in light of addressing the non-comparative (or "basic") needs of the laborers; what is illustrated here, consequently, is how acts of mercy are in accord with non-comparative justice.[14]

Similar to the householder, the Good Samaritan does what is right or just in giving the battered traveler his due. The summary formula that captures the spirit of this ethic is that persons should love one another (including themselves) as God loves them; in doing so, one gives others (and oneself) their due: recognition as a being unto death and in need of redemption which comes only through the faithful acknowledgement and acceptance of God's love. To treat persons out of hate, in anger, or with indifference is to deny their deepest need that can be satisfied only through being embraced by "God's love in us" which calls the other to salvation.[15]

Notes

1. As Radcliffe acknowledges, "ought implies can," and one who is not loving cannot be commanded to love another "directly" but, if becoming loving is within his scope of possibility, then he has the responsibility to do what is required to become a loving person. This is akin to the addict that now may not be able to directly will sobriety but who can choose to take the necessary steps (enter into a rehabilitation program and so forth) to become sober. On this issue, Kant claims in *The Metaphysics of Morals*:

So the saying 'you ought to love your neighbor as yourself' does not mean that you ought immediately (first) to love him and (afterwards) by means of this love to do good to him. It means rather, *do good* to your fellow human beings, and your beneficence will produce love of them in you (as an aptitude of the inclination to beneficence in general). (Kant, 1996:531)

So, even if a particular person of "normal" capacities of rational self-control were not capable of becoming a compassionate person who spontaneously acts for the benefit of others, such person would nevertheless be capable of acting in accordance with the principle of compassion.

2. For a discussion of the "pure precepts" see Loori (1996:Chs. 6-8). The "third" pure precept of "Actualizing Good for Others" applies more to one's responsibilities to fellow spiritual practitioners (*sangha*) than to others generally, for whom we are to follow the "second" pure precept of "Practicing Good." Regarding the priority of the pure precepts, the Dalai Lama proclaims: "I like to say that the essence of the Buddha's teaching can be found in two sayings: If possible, you should help others. If that is not possible, at least you should do no harm. Refraining from harming others is the essence of the initial stage of living the teachings of morality." (Dalai Lama, 2002:70-71)

3. See Chapter I, endnote # 6 and Richard Taylor (1985:167).

4. It should be noted that Schweitzer rejected the idea that compassion constitutes the sole ground of morality, of "reverence for life." After noting, "Ethics are responsibility without limit towards all that lives," he remarks:

Compassion is too narrow to rank as the essence of the ethical. It denotes, of course, only interest in the suffering will-to-live. But ethics include also feeling as one's own in all circumstances and all the aspirations of the will-to-live, its pleasure, too, and its longing to live life to the full, as well as the urge to self-perfecting. (Schweitzer, 1960:311)

Schweitzer's point is well taken. In Mahāyāna practice, "compassion" is one of four "boundless qualities"--the others being love, sympathetic joy, and equanimity--that are to be integrated in life; and, we should not forget, that one's compassion embraces one's "freedom" to live each moment fully. In short, one should take a broad view on what is embraced by the "well being" of oneself and others that is to be nurtured, promoted and protected. It is with this broad view that the Dalai Lama proclaims: "...compassion is one of the principal things that make our lives meaningful. It is the source of all lasting happiness and joy. And it is the foundation of a good heart, the heart of one who acts out of a desire to help others." (Dalai Lama, 1999:234)

5. Buddhists generally hold that all living beings have a moral history as well as the potential for spiritual liberation; but, it seems to me, even if this is challenged, one can resort to the other four elements as constituting a "living being." See King, 1994. The resultant view of a "living being" has a long pedigree in the West. Aristotle's notion of an animal is that of a being requiring nourishment which also is capable of sensation (perception) and desire (appetite); these capacities are unified in one organ, the heart. The aim of all animal behavior is "well being" which includes not only persistence in living but in flourishing according to the potential of the species to which the animal belongs. See *De Anima*, Bk. III, 11-12 and Stephen Everson (1995). Because Aristotelian animals are capable of feeling pleasure and pain, and since animals both desire their own well-being and can be frustrated in that desire, animals are capable of suffering in the sense

appropriate for moral "considerability" from the perspective of an ethic of compassion. Jack Wilson's analysis (1999) provides conceptual support, from the vantage of contemporary biological science. Wilson (1999:60) distinguishes six criteria on the basis of which one might answer the question of whether some living entity is an "individual." Of the six, the most crucial for our purposes is that of function. Functional individuality implies that the parts of which an entity are composed are causally integrated into a functional unit; but, what makes a sentient being a "functional unit" is its capability of persistence in living, unless it is *"subsumed into a higher-level entity or parasitized"* (p. 99, emphases in original text), in which case it becomes a functional part of another biological entity. That "life" or "living well" is the end of the behavior of living beings is captured by Spinoza's notion of "conatus" in his *Ethics* as well by Schopenhauer's "will-to-live" in *The World as Will and Representation*.

6. Plato, *Republic*, I, 332a-b, trans. by W.C. Cornford. Plato clearly associated, e.g., in the *Gorgias*, "acting unjustly" with "acting wrongly" and with "causing harm."

7. For a profound view on "impartiality," see Patrul Rinpoche, 1998:195-234. To treat others impartially is not to treat others necessarily as "the same" or as "equals." Damien Keown (1992:98-99) points out, for example, according to Buddhaghosa, "animals" are not "equal" to "humans" and that not all humans are equal on the criterion of "sanctity." Nevertheless, I think that we treat beings impartially by not relating to them through our personal "attachments;" and we act impartially in intending to achieve the greatest possible good (i.e., reducing the amount of suffering as much as possible).

8. A well known Christian ethicist claims:

> Justice is Christian love using its head, calculating its duties, obligations, opportunities, resources....Justice is love coping with situations where distribution is called for. On this basis it becomes plain that as the love ethic searches seriously for a social policy it must form a coalition with utilitarianism. It takes over from Bentham and Mill the strategic principle of "the greatest good for the greatest number." (Joseph Fletcher, 1966:95)

If one remains at the level of social policy, this standpoint has some merit. But, the notion that individuals' moral choices should be grounded on a utilitarian principle cannot be accepted as consistent with Buddhist practice nor with the notion of universal compassion. See Damien Keown, 1992:Ch. 7. We will return to this issue in Ch. IV.6.

9. The nature and scope of the "latitude" of Kantian imperfect duties have received enormous attention over the past few decades. For an overview of this topic along with a helpful bibliography, see Baron, 1995, esp. chapters 3 and 5. In the end, Baron (following Thomas Hill) holds that the Kantian imperfect duty of beneficence requires one to adopt a maxim to promote the happiness of others, from which it follows that (a) it is mandatory to promote the happiness of others *sometimes*, perhaps including occasions in which another's life is in danger and when to help would require little sacrifice, but (b) there is never an occasion in which one is morally required to exercise that duty in lieu of a perfect duty that requires one to act otherwise instead.

More recently, Allen Wood has argued:

> The notion that Kantian ethics is committed to strict exceptionless rules because it regards moral principles as categorical imperatives is based on the crudest misunderstanding. A categorical imperative is unconditional in the sense that its rational validity does not presuppose any end given independently

of that imperative, that is to be reached by following it. But this is far from im-
plying that the obligatoriness of particular moral rules or duties is unconditional. For instance, respect for rational nature might normally require compliance with a certain rule, but there could well be conditions under which it does
not, and under those conditions the rule would simply not be a categorical imperative at all. (Wood, 2008:63)

Wood might well think that the analysis I provide below is one consistent with Kantian
ethics, for he sees Kant as open to the exercise of "judgment" in complying with one's
duties; yet, to say that one has "good" reason to forego fulfilling a perfect duty on some
occasion is not sufficient, it seems to me, to provide a sound basis for explaining when
one's reasons are "good enough."

Moreover, that perfect duties should trump imperfect or wide duties seems to be
required by Kant's project to provide a unified moral theory that covers both juridical
duties and ethical duties. The system of juridical duties functions to protect the external
freedom of persons in doing, as we would say, "what they have a right to do" (thereby
respecting their humanity as ends-in-themselves) by externally constraining their violation through "enforcement" or (threats of) punishment. Kant's distinction between "perfect" and "imperfect" duties allows him to maintain that violations of juridical duties
cannot be "justified" or "excused" on the grounds of one's "ethical duty." In short, Kant
did not accept legal defenses of "necessity" or "justification," as illustrated in Aquinas'
case (discussed below, p.62) of the person who is in "imminent danger" and takes another's property to succor his own needs or in the case where a parent so acts to succor
the needs of a starving child. (See Rosen, 1993:104-5)

10. What the relationship is between juridical duties and perfect ethical duties (of
virtue) is a matter of some controversy among Kant scholars. While Wood holds that it is
incorrect to think that Kant derives the universal law of justice from the supreme principle of morality, e.g., the categorical imperative, nevertheless, he holds: "Every juridical
duty, however, for Kant counts also as an ethical duty, in the sense that the worth of humanity, which grounds ethics, requires us also to respect the right." (Wood, 2008:162)
Since both juridical duties and ethical duties belong to "morality," I think it reasonable to
hold that both classes of duties have moral justification only on the basis of the supreme
principle of morality; otherwise, we are in need of an independent account of "legal obligation" and this Kant was not prepared to offer. (Rosen, 1993:111-14)

11. I refer here to the *Groundwork of the Metaphysics of Morals*, 4:423 (Kant,
1996a:74-75), where Kant presents the "fourth" illustration of his supreme principle of
morality. Allen Wood claims that it is the duty of sympathy—what he refers to as the
duty of "sympathetic participation"—rather than the duty of beneficence that is here being illustrated. (Wood, 2008:177) Wood characterizes Kant's duty of sympathetic participation as "the active sharing in the situation of another, seeing things from their point of
view, which will then give rise both to compassionate feelings and to beneficent actions."
(Wood, 2008:176-77) Kant disparages "compassion" and "pity" precisely because these
"feelings" are not sufficient to motivate beneficent actions. For our purposes, it does not
matter whether we see the "duty of beneficence*" as comparable to Kant's "duty of beneficence" or to his "duty of sympathetic participation" that yields on appropriate occasions beneficent actions.

12. Kant held that one has the duty to act from duty, meaning that one acts from an
"inner constraint" to do one's duty. It might make sense, given this, to say that the moral
worth of the agent's doing what accords with duty is that it be done from duty, from inner

constraint. But two points should be emphasized here. To say that one's doing the right thing "spontaneously" or "naturally," hence not from (an inner constraint of) duty, does not have "moral worth" for Kant does not imply that what the agent did does not have moral value. (Wood, 2008:26-32) Secondly, it might happen that the "spontaneity" with which one now does the right thing results from one's having followed one's duty to perfect himself morally by cultivating such virtues as "sympathetic participation." What then? Might not the agent deserve to be esteemed for becoming the sort of person who, at least on some occasions, quite effortlessly and spontaneously does what accords with duty?

In an exceptionally lucid commentary, David Gallagher argues that for Aquinas, "moral goodness" is located "in acts of the will, in acts such as choice, intention, or consent;" and that "moral goodness" can be applied analogously to both the "agent" as well as to the "exterior act" (conduct). (Gallagher, 1994:55-58) In so far as in one's conduct one intends to not harm others but to do good for others, one's conduct will be "morally good," other things being equal, and one will show oneself to be a "good person." However, the further point is stressed by both Aquinas and Kant that unless it is a genuinely "good will" that underlies one's intentionality, and this requires that one has the "virtues" necessary to effectively direct oneself to do what is right (for the right reasons), particular examples of doing "good acts" may not reflect a genuinely "good person" (or a person with a genuinely "good will").

13. Standard commentaries on the Parable of Laborers in the Vineyard take the landowner as representing God and, hence, aim to justify the landowner's norm of comparative justice. See, for example, Lebacqz (1983), who analyzes the parable in light of several interpretations of the norm of comparative justice from the perspective that the landowner represents God. Alternatively, if one does not assume that the landowner represents God, then one may see the parable as a criticism of the "elitist" norm of comparative justice then prevalent. (E.g., Herzog, 1994) While Herzog (among others) provides some ground for taking a *denarius* to represent "subsistence," neither he nor other commentators he cites view the parable as illustrating a *justified norm of noncomparative justice*. The most illuminating analysis I know of the teachings of Jesus within a framework of "compassion" is Drengston, 1981.

14. That there is no incompatibility between "mercy" and "justice" in God is argued for by Thomas Aquinas, *ST*, II-II, Q. 21 and, more recently, by Talbott, 1993.

15. For a particularly striking illustration of what might be called "redemptive justice," see the story of Francis of Assisi and Brother Angelo and "the murderous robbers." (Ugolino, 1958:100-01) While the three vagabonds, by virtue of their criminal deeds and the norms of comparative or retributive justice, deserve to be punished by the state, and perhaps deserve to be ostracized by their community, it is clear that Francis directed Angelo to relate to them in light of their humanity and their needs for compassion and redemption. Michael Blastic (2000) provides an insightful account of how this episode illustrates "attentive compassion."

Chapter IV
Precepts for Avoiding Doing Evil

It can be seen with a little reflection that the precepts gesture beyond themselves in the direction of certain values which it is their function to preserve. Their formulation as negative injunctions flashes an alert that anyone contemplating such actions as killing or stealing is threatening an assault on certain values or 'goods.'

Damien Keown, *Buddhism and Bioethics*

Thomas Aquinas defines "law" as "nothing else than an ordinance of reason for the common good, made by him who has care of the community, and promulgated." (*ST*, I-II, Q. 90, Art. 4) On Aquinas's view, a law is imposed "as a rule and a measure" on beings who are to be "ruled and measured" by it. The source of "law" is a "superior being" who has the authority to rule and measure other beings. In the case of civil law, the State or the Sovereign rules and measures its citizens; in the case of the moral law, on Aquinas's view, it is God who "rules and measures" human beings in accordance with moral laws (e.g., the "Commandments") which have been promulgated to us. Hence, moral rules such as "One ought not to kill" or "One ought not to steal" or, even, "Love Thy Neighbor" are "commands" that issue from a superior authority who "rules and measures" the members of the moral community. R.M. Hare (1964, 1965) has argued that the "imperative" nature of moral rules is part of the "logic" of moral language. Perhaps this is true within Western culture, but the notion of a "moral precept" to be developed here has different roots and a different "logic."

As we have seen, that one is "to do good" and "to avoid evil" is to be understood in light of the notion of suffering: one ought not to cause unnecessary suffering but, instead, where possible, relieve and protect beings from suffering. In cultivating compassion, it is essential that one not only identifies with others in a general way, but that one understands deeply the nature of the sufferings of beings whom one encounters. To effectively (help to) relieve others' sufferings requires great insight, determination, and perseverance; after all, one must understand that the other suffers, why the other suffers and what is required to alleviate efficiently the other's suffering; and then one must apply the remedy! The aim of reflecting on one's own and others' vulnerabilities to suffering is to achieve openness and insight which, together, engender intelligent responsiveness. As Blum remarks, "it is not merely that the sympathetic person perceives things differently from the sympathy-less person, but also that he perceives things more accurately, with more insight." (Blum, 1980b:135) This might come quite "naturally" through one's thorough familiarity with other beings: parents with children, animal lovers with pets, experienced gardeners with plants, and so on. What distinguishes the cultivation of compassion from these kinds of sensitivities is simply the lack of a compartmentalized concern for one or another kind of being.

In an ethics of compassion, as we shall see, moral "precepts" can be derived from the two principles of acting compassionately: "I ought not to cause any living beings to suffer unnecessarily" and "I ought to relieve/protect other living beings from unnecessary suffering." Since these principles are in the "first person" and are reached by an intelligent being's own reflection, they do not originate "outside" one's self. Therefore, the precepts that are derived from these principles also are stated in the first person—they are not "general rules" that can function as imperatives or commands promulgated by some "higher" authority, even, as for Kant, universal "reason." The precepts that can be derived from the principle of moral obligation are negative in formulation and hence are akin to "prohibitions;" I call them "precepts for avoiding doing evil (harm)." We will examine five such precepts in this chapter. Our examinations of them individually will uncover a number of general aspects or dimensions that characterize all such precepts. Corresponding to each "negative" precept of obligation, a "positive" formulation can be derived from the principle of moral aspiration; these "prescriptions" or "aspirations" will be discussed in the next chapter.[1] Our consideration of how these precepts do function, including the conditions under which they admit to "exceptions," makes clear how an ethic of compassion differs from standard Western normative theories, e.g., utilitarianism, Kantian formalism, natural law theory and care ethics.

1. The First Precept: I Refrain from the Taking of Life

"The First Precept," a mindfulness-training on the preciousness of life, can be derived from our preceding line of reasoning (1)-(5) as follows:

5.   I ought not to cause any human (living) beings to suffer unnecessarily.

6. To intentionally kill a human (living) being is to cause that being unnecessary suffering.[2]
7. Therefore, I ought not to kill intentionally any human (living) being;
   that is, I ought to refrain from taking life.

In vowing to practice the so-called "precepts of right action," one vows to
abstain from *intentionally* engaging in certain kinds of conduct that are bound to
cause unnecessary suffering. Thus, the First Precept proscribes, in the words of
Hammalawa Saddhatissa one's intentionally "destroying, causing to be destroyed, or sanctioning the destruction of a living being." (Saddhatissa, 1977:59)
On the matter of killing *intentionally*, Saddhatissa expresses the standard Buddhist view as follows.

> There are five conditions that constitute the immoral act of killing: (1) the fact
> and presence of a living being, human or animal; (2) the knowledge that the be-
> ing is a living being; (3) the intent or resolution to kill; (4) the act of killing by
> appropriate means; and (5) the resulting death. In the absence of any one of
> these conditions, the act would not constitute killing even though death should
> follow; the event would be considered an accident (Saddhatissa, 1977:60)

While we might fault one for having "wrongful attitudes," including certainly a
desire or wish for the death of a living being, one's merely having such a desire
or wish does not violate the First Precept as formulated above, although expressing such a desire or wish might if doing so contributes foreseeably to the death
of a living being.

One might think that the First Precept only establishes a "rule of thumb" or
a *prima facie* duty to abstain from taking life or even the life of a human being.
Are there not other duties that may conflict with and override this one?
Or, might not one find oneself in a situation where one can protect an innocent
life only by taking (the aggressor's) life? What then? To pursue this line of inquiry, let us examine an illustrative case in which it might be thought that intentional killing of a human being is justified.

Imagine a situation in which an enraged father seeks revenge on someone
who he thinks raped and killed his daughter. It turns out that the father is planning to kill your brother, whom he wrongly believes is the culprit. You learn of
your brother's endangerment and arrive at his house just as the father is about to
launch lit sticks of dynamite through the window of the room where your
brother is watching television. Do you have the right to shoot at the father with
the intention of killing him in order to save your brother's life?

Is killing in defense of an "innocent" person a morally correct action?
First, a note on what constitutes a "morally correct" action. I shall understand
this to refer to an action that, if performed, does not leave the agent open to the
charge of failing to have done his duty by not doing some alternative action that
the agent should reasonably be expected to have considered. Now, we often
hear, "Killing is wrong except in self-defense" and "Killing is wrong except

when it is necessary to save an innocent person's life." Since, what I am interested in determining is whether there are exceptions to the First Precept that prohibits the intentional taking of life, the issue I wish to focus on is whether intentional killing is morally correct in cases either of self defense or of saving an innocent person's life. There is no question that one has the right to 'protect' either oneself or an "innocent" person. Further, one has the right to use "force" in providing protection. In case (1), for example, throwing a rock at the enraged father--hoping to distract him or to hit him so that he misses his target when letting go of the dynamite--would be permissible. It would even be permissible to aim the gun to wound the father, again with the motive of preventing him from finding his target. But these actions, even if they were to cause the father's death, for example by his dropping the lit explosives which then explode at his own feet, would not be in violation of the First Precept since they are not done with the intention or resolution to kill the father. The death so caused is "accidental."

What my illustrative case proposes is that you think that you might save your brother by killing the would-be assailant and, hence, you fire the gun with precisely the intention of killing him. To make the situation even more compelling, we might add that you reasonably believe that, should the would-be assailant not be killed on this occasion, then he would not rest until he got his full revenge. Is intentional killing here morally correct? An ethic of compassion bids us to frame the issue this way: how is it that we show compassion for someone by intending to kill him? Is not to intentionally kill someone to cause that person a great, unnecessary suffering? One might reflect, "Am I acting toward the enraged father with the same degree of compassion that I have for my brother or which I would show to my own spouse, child or parent? If my brother were the one with the lit dynamite, would I intend to kill him rather than merely attempt to prevent him from achieving his murderous aim? If I were in the position of the enraged father, could I will that someone intend to kill me as a means to save a potential victim rather than to act out of concern for both the potential victim and myself?" (Note: it does not matter here whether the potential victim is "innocent" or not in terms of the harm caused to the would-be assassin.)[3]

Is intentional killing, then, ever justified? The First Precept is an expression of compassion; if one's compassion for another (human) being requires one to kill that being in order to protect or relieve it from unnecessary suffering, then killing fulfills the spirit of the First Precept. I relate two examples. The first is offered by Roshi Daido Loori.

> From the perspective of compassion and reverence for life, one should be clear that this ["first"] precept means to refrain from killing the mind of compassion and reverence. Also, and this is a very subtle point, an aspect of observing this precept includes killing with the sword of compassion when necessary. Several years ago I was driving along the highway and a raccoon walked out under the wheels of my car. I ran over it. It was pretty young, badly crushed, and crying out in terrible pain. My own self-centeredness, squeamishness, and fear prevented me from taking its life and putting it out of its misery. I could have just

driven the car back over it. But I could not bring myself to do that. I left it on the highway and drove away. In doing so, I killed the mind of compassion and reverence for life that was inside me. I violated the precept "Do not kill" because I did not have the heart to kill that raccoon. My own feelings were more important than the agony of the creature. (Loori, 1996: 85-86)

The second example relies on a context of karma, but its point is similar. In Buddhist practice, a specific exception is made to the First Precept for the *bodhisattva* so to permit the "[t]aking the life of someone about to commit an act entailing immediate retribution...in order to prevent them [sic] suffering the evil consequences of that act." (Keown, 1992:143) In this kind of case, the *bodhisattva*, out of compassion, kills another about, say, to murder her parent, not in order to save the life of the intended victim but out of compassion for the would-be assailant. For, if one murders her parent, one would cause one's self many times the karmic suffering than what would be caused by the destruction of her life.

One way of putting the matter is that one may understand the First Precept to mean, "One ought not to kill another living being since one should treat all beings in the most compassionate way possible." From this it follows that should a situation arise in which it is only by killing a living being that one can treat *that* being in the most compassionate way possible, then one would fulfill the duty of compassion that grounds the First Precept precisely by violating the precept. Notice then that the precept against killing is not *prima facie* in the sense that it can be overridden by another *prima facie* precept; rather the precept against the taking of life can only be overridden by the application of the very *principle* that the precept embodies. Furthermore, since "exceptions" to precepts are rare in the course of one's life, it would be misleading to take the First Precept as a "rule of thumb." Unless we are confident in our discernment, we act correctly in following the First Precept without exception.[4]

2. The Second Precept: I Refrain from Taking What is not Given

The Second Precept may be reached as follows:

5. I ought not to cause any human (living) being to suffer unnecessarily.
6a. To take intentionally from a human (living) being what it needs to live or to prosper is to cause that being to suffer unnecessarily.
7a. Therefore, I ought to refrain from taking (from a human/living being) what is not given.

Of course, the usual way to refer to this injunction is to say, "One ought not to steal." Generally, it is harmful to steal what belongs to others; the goods stolen might have contributed to the livelihood or well-being of the owner; the victim also suffers a violation of security that increases his and the general community's mistrust and fear of others. And, most usually, the person who steals does not benefit in the long run; undisciplined greed and self-centeredness bring one considerable suffering in the way of not being content with what one has and by others' lack of trust and friendship. However, the Second Precept states a moral obligation or mindfulness training that is very general and not bound to or by legal conventions regarding "property" and "legal entitlements" as the following cases illustrate.

Consider first this situation raised by Thomas Aquinas:

> Nevertheless, if the need be so manifest and urgent, that it is evident that the present need must be remedied by whatever means be at hand (for instance, when a person is in some imminent danger, and there is no other possible remedy), then it is lawful for a man to succor his own need by means of another's property, by taking it either openly or secretly; nor is this properly speaking theft or robbery. (Aquinas, *ST*, II-II, Q. 66, Art 7)

This passage follows Aquinas's point that there is "a duty of charity" for a person with an *abundance* of goods to share with those in dire need. In this light, if one fails out of charity to share from his abundance, then, it might seem, he has no moral right to what he holds back, and, hence, for a desperately needy individual to take (from) it would not constitute robbery, strictly speaking. But suppose that the needy person were to take the only available food from another person's family, thus reducing them to a state of "immediate danger of physical privation." In this case, we would seem to have a clear violation of the Second Precept, while in the case of superabundance we do not. Whereas "necessity" justifies a taking from another in the former case, for Aquinas, it would not even excuse such a taking in the latter for one who accepts the Second Precept.

In commenting on the Second Precept, Robert Aitken observes:

> Stealing is a pervasive element of our lives, and is the nature of our economic system. 'The rich get rich (sic) and the poor get poorer.' To take an extreme example, a large American corporation raises vegetables in the Sahel, near the Sahara Desert. These vegetables are flown to Europe, where they fill the salad bowls of the affluent. The African workers on this giant farm, whose families and friends are on the edge of starvation, are searched at the end of each day to be sure they are not smuggling vegetables home. Yet the corporation land they cultivate was once their own for gleaning and grazing. (Aitken, 1984:29-30)

Or consider as a third type of case the depletion of rain forests in South America due to commercial timbering, mining and agriculture. The short-term consequences of this destruction are catastrophic for many species of wildlife and plants; and, the long-term effects on the environment, due to global warming for instance, could prove quite harmful for human beings as well. Regardless of "legal entitlements," such an appropriation of natural resources, precisely because of foreseeable, consequential suffering to living beings, would violate the Second Precept. Some people regard the commercialization of such products as honey to violate the precept as well since it involves a taking of what is not given of a substance vital to the well being of living beings. (Harvey, 2000:165) The Second Precept, along with the First, extends well beyond the human community and is integral to "an environmental ethic."

These three cases illustrate two themes. First, what constitutes "taking what is not given" is not to be construed within the parameters of legal or institutional conventions. It largely is irrelevant whether the individual with stores of abundance, or his neighbor in desperate need, or the African farm hands, or even the bees for that matter, "own" or can claim a "right" to the resources at hand necessary for survival and prosperity. Second, one may violate the Second Precept directly or indirectly; for instance, not only the person who harvests and sells honey, or who grows, markets and sells the African vegetables, "takes what is not given" but so too does the consumer, although perhaps not intentionally. On the other hand, whether one "violates" the Second Precept in one's consumer habits, or in the more direct ways of "stealing" and "fraud" we are so familiar with, is itself a recognition of the "the mind of compassion" within oneself, as Roshi Loorie pointed out in disclosing his own sense of violating the precept against killing.

3. The Third Precept: I Refrain from Sexual Misconduct

Again, a familiar pattern of reasoning can be instantiated.

5.   I ought not to cause any human (living) being to suffer unnecessarily.
6b. Sexual misconduct harms human (living) beings unnecessarily.
7b. I ought to refrain from sexual misconduct.

It is compassion that is expressed in the precepts and Schopenhauer observed how, for the person acting with compassion, "the barrier between ego and non-ego is for the moment abolished." (Schopenhauer, 1995:165-66) The lack of compassion, on the other hand, normally is an expression of self-centeredness; and, sexual relations which gratify one's self, which gravitate around one's own ego-needs, which, therefore, do not focus on the long-term good of the other, constitute misconduct. This is not only exemplified in the most obviously exploitive forms of sexual behavior: rape, sexual abuse of minors, prostitution, sexual harassment of employees, and the like, but also in many of the various forms of consensual liaisons and affairs to which we are tempted.

It is difficult to specify the conditions for non-harmful sexual relations, or, even, the conditions under which one might intentionally engage in non-harmful sexual relations. It is common for philosophers to take the view that since no one wishes to harm oneself, mutual, free and informed consent among adults is sufficient to preclude non-harmfulness. But, this assumes that the parties consenting are not deluded about their own best interests. So, one might opt for a higher standard: yes, free and informed mutual consent, but with a genuine concern for the well being of one another, not just "now" but in the future as well. It really does not matter if sexual unions that genuinely meet this standard are heterosexual or homosexual or whether they are monogamous or polygamous; and, while public vows might express more fully and deeply the nature of shared commitments, it is not the formality of a ceremony that seems to be essential. In working on understanding and expressing one's profound capacities to love another person, within the context of the pure intentionality of compassion, as free as possible from ego attachments, one guides oneself by the Third Precept.

It even might happen that, given an extraordinary set of circumstances, the spirit of Third Precept is honored by short-term sexual encounters. This is illustrated by Joseph Fletcher's case of "sacrificial adultery" in the aftermath of WW II. A German father had been picked up by the Allied armies in Germany and sent off to Wales and shortly thereafter the Russian army seized his wife, Mrs. Bergmeier, who was foraging for food with her three children, and sent her to a prison camp in the Ukraine. Her husband returned to Germany and rounded up the children; during this time, her only thought was to "reknit them as a family in that dire situation of hunger, chaos, and fear."

> Meanwhile, in the Ukraine, Mrs. Bergmeier learned through a sympathetic commandant that her husband and family were trying to keep together and find her. But the rules allowed them to release her for only two reasons: (1) illness needing medical facilities beyond the camp's, in which case she would be sent to a Soviet hospital elsewhere, and (2) pregnancy, in which she could be returned to Germany as a liability. She turned things over in her mind and finally asked a friendly Volga German camp guard to impregnate her, which he did. Her condition being medically verified, she was sent back to Berlin and her family. They welcomed her with open arms, even when she told them how she did it. When the child was born, they loved him more than all the rest, on the view that little Dietrich had done more for them than anybody. (Fletcher, 1966:164-65)

4. The Fourth Precept: I Refrain from Verbal Transgressions

"Sticks and stones may break my bones, but names will never hurt me!" may express one's stoical resolve not to be defeated by verbal abuse, but, in fact, words often do harm us as well as hurt us. There are four types of "verbal transgressions" that cause harm unnecessarily: (a) lying, (b) duplicity, (c) harsh words, and (d) idle talk. (Hsing Yun, 1998:15-20) The recognition of wrongful or harmful speech underlies the Third Precept.

5. I ought not to cause any human (living) being to suffer unnecessarily.
6c. Verbal transgressions cause human (living) beings to suffer unnecessarily.
7c. Therefore, I ought to refrain from verbal transgressions.

While this prohibition covers well familiar territory for anyone who has thought through the meaning of "One ought not to lie," it extends to some less familiar territory as well.

Lying is harmful generally since it adds to the delusion in which others operate, and delusion or ignorance is one of the primary sources of suffering; lying often underlies an exploitation of others; in addition, lying erodes trust in others as well as confidence in one's own intuitions.

> When we say something that we know is not true we have committed an overt lie. When we fail to say something that we know that we should say, we have committed a lie of omission. A lie of omission may be more subtle than an overt lie, but it is no less serious. If the intention is to harm someone or not prevent someone from harming themselves, a lie of omission can be very serious. (Hsing Yun, 1998:16-17)

Duplicity includes the various pretentious ways in which we fail to communicate fully who we are, where we stand, and what we feel. Flattery, posturing, hypocrisy, and pursuing "hidden agenda" fall within the scope of duplicity as well as efforts to sow discord within the community.

Harsh speech includes the grossest "verbal abuse" to the subtlest "put-downs" and "criticisms" that undermine self-confidence and self-worth. Often "blame" is not salutary; although to gently point out to someone the harmfulness of his or her conduct, while not pleasant or easy, can be of great benefit. Finally, idle talk includes "gossip" which might be "truthful" but spoken at the wrong times with a lack of compassion for those about whom one speaks. It also includes pointless speech which has no value to others and wastes their time or distracts them from more beneficial pursuits. Most "bitch" sessions over morning coffee sow and nourish harmful seeds of discord.

Roshi Loorie illustrated how one's compassion and reverence for life that underlies a commitment to the First Precept might require a killing of an animal in a particular circumstance just as it proscribes the taking of life generally, so, too, at times, the truth may be served by speech that appears "dishonest" or "harsh." Let us consider again the case of the enraged father who seeks revenge on someone, your brother, who he mistakenly thinks raped and killed his daughter. Suppose, armed with rage and a weapon, he asks if your brother has taken refuge in your home? Knowing that he is in no mood for edifying moral discourse but only for a direct answer, what should you say? Most of us would wish to mislead the enraged father out of loving concern for our brother. At the same time, in this case, since the enraged father already is acting with the illusion of false belief, to mislead him is not to further lead him away from the truth; indeed, once he calms down and can reflect on the evidence at hand, he will see that the person he suspected was not the rapist-killer. So, to enable him to "see the truth before it is too late" one might need *first* to say what is literally not true in order for the truth to be revealed.

This theme is illustrated with respect to "harsh speech" in a well known story:

> A big burly samurai comes to the wise man and says, 'Tell me the nature of heaven and hell.' And the roshi looks at him in the face and says, "Why should I tell a scruffy, disgusting, miserable slob like you?' The samurai starts to get purple in the face, his hair starts to stand up, but the roshi won't stop, he keeps saying, 'A miserable worm like you, do you think that I should tell you anything?' Consumed by rage, the samurai draws his sword, and he's just about to cut off the head of the roshi. Then the roshi says, 'That's hell.' The samurai, who is in fact a sensitive person, instantly gets it, that he has just created his own hell; he was deep in hell. It was black and hot, filled with hatred, self-protection, anger, and resentment, so much so that he was going to kill this man. Tears fill his eyes and he starts to cry and he puts his palms together and the roshi says, 'That's heaven.' (Pema Chödrön, 1991:29)

While "harsh speech" has the potential to cause great harm, it might be a skillful means to conveying, compassionately, a most important truth.

5. The Fifth Precept: I Refrain from Harmful Consumption

Aware of the suffering caused by unmindful consumption, I am committed to cultivating good health, both physical and mental, for myself, my family, and my society by practicing mindful eating, drinking, and consuming.

Thich Nhat Hanh, *Touching Peace*, 89

Thich Nhat Hanh here points out that people in the West tend to think that their bodies belong to themselves alone and, hence, from a certain age, they may treat them any way they wish; indeed, social mores and the law seem to reinforce this attitude. Moreover, some philosophers hold that the very notion of "duties to oneself" is incoherent. Nevertheless, we know that, often, one's consumption patterns are harmful not only to oneself but to others as well. The Fifth Precept historically focused on "intoxicants" like alcohol and opium. Ingesting such substances, especially addictively, often interferes with one's ability to discharge family and social responsibilities; mind-altered states can result in dangerous or harmful behaviors as they interfere with one's clearly and diligently following the aforementioned precepts. Of course, it is not just alcohol and drugs that "cloud" the mind and have harmful consequences. Consumerism, racism, sexism, and violence-as-problem solver are just a few of the attitudes that are "consumed" daily through the mass media, including music, cinema, and television.

If one recognizes the potential that one's unmindful consumption has for harmfully affecting others, then one may reason to the Fifth Precept as follows.

5. I ought not to cause any human (living) being to suffer unnecessarily.
6d. Behaviors under the influence of intoxicants or false views cause human (living) beings to suffer unnecessarily.
6d'. Harmful consumption is to become intoxicated or infected with false views.
7d. I ought to refrain from harmful consumption.

Living in the spirit of this precept involves a great deal of thoughtfulness and judgment. I do not think that it requires one to abstain totally from all substances which have the potential to intoxicate or infect one, but, at least, to refrain from becoming intoxicated or infected in such a way that one is likely to cause harm (to oneself or others) unnecessarily. My friend Sam visits his elderly mother for a week several times a year. His mother is increasingly reclusive but mentally quite sharp, loquacious, and looks forward to long talks with Sam. It is her habit to take a nap in the late afternoon, after which she is particularly energized for a good conversation. Sam finds that he is a much better listener and conversationalist if he has a "fine" Scotch or two before dinner; he transforms a potential poison into an elixir.

6. Moral Rules: A Middle Way

If we take *only* the kinds of cases illustrated above as constituting legitimate "exceptions" to the literal expression of precepts, then whether and when there are "exceptions to rules of obligation" are issues determined much differently within an ethics of compassion than within the frameworks of (Kantian) formalism, natural law theory, care ethics, or utilitarianism.

As we saw in Chapter III, Kantian formalism normally is understood as not permitting any exceptions to so-called "perfect duties" which may be expressed as "objective maxims" and include, at least, prohibitions of murder, stealing, lying and sexual misconduct in a variety of forms. Natural law ethics forbids one's intentionally violating "a basic human good" such as "life," "justice," "knowledge" or "truth." On this view, an intentional act of killing a human being would violate the good of "life;" an intentional act of stealing or a willful failure not to repay a loan would violate the good of "justice;" to intentionally lie would violate the good of "truth;" and to secretly carry on an adulterous affair would violate the goods of "justice" and "truth" as well as, perhaps, the basic good of "family." So, in effect, natural law theory, on some interpretations, finds moral absolutes at least in some of the same places as does Kantian for-

malism, under some interpretations. An ethic of compassion rejects moral absolutes on a two-fold ground: situations may arise in which the principle of compassion, on which the precept is based, is contravened by following the precept;
and, in some such situations, the option of non-action would be a willful failure
to relieve/protect beings from unnecessary and serious suffering (without directly causing unnecessary and serious suffering).

At the other extreme, an ethic of caring views moral responsibilities as extending only to those with whom one is in (potential) "relationship;" care is inherently "partial" and extends to those with whom one has relationships and not
to all others "universally" or "impartially." On this type of view, one may feel it
necessary to kill or otherwise harm others in order to "protect" those for whom
one cares. Nel Noddings explains:

> While I must not kill in obedience to law or principle, I may not, either, refuse
> to kill in obedience to principle. To remain one-caring, I might have to kill.
> Consider the case of a woman who kills her sleeping husband. Under most cir-
> cumstances, the one-caring would judge such an act wrong. It violates the very
> possibility of caring for the husband. But as she hears how the husband abused
> his wife and children, about the fear with which the woman lived, about the
> past efforts to solve the problem legally, the one-caring revises her judgment.
> The jury finds the woman not guilty by reason of extenuated self-defense. The
> one-caring finds her ethical, but under a sadly diminished ethical ideal. (Nod-
> dings, 1984:102)

The ethical question here is, did the abused wife act responsibly, *justifiably*, in
killing her husband?; not whether she acted excusably. On one view the answer
is, "Yes, she acted justifiably since her responsibility as one-caring is to herself
and her family members with whom she is in a relationship of reciprocity and
respect, if not, yet, full mutuality, and not to one who aggresses harmfully
against those individuals." Notice, too, that this stance is not made on act-
utilitarian grounds, since there is no attempt to "weigh" the utilities of various
courses of action open to the abused woman and to do that act that has the highest foreseeable utility. Indeed, if the husband were the head of state or the head
of a medical-research team on the verge of an important public health discovery,
the wife's killing him would decidedly not have utilitarian justification, but this
would be of little concern to "one-caring." Interestingly, the ethic of compassion
herein advocated views the obligation not to intentionally cause another unnecessary suffering as being paramount and, hence, would agree with the stances of
natural law theory and Kantian formalism in judging the battered-wife's taking
of human life as unethical.

In *The Nature of Buddhist Ethics*, Keown remarks:

> In many ways the Mahāyāna concept of Skilful Means (*upāya-kauśalya*) seems
> susceptible to analysis along AU [act-utilitarian] lines since rules are frequently
> disregarded if the subsequent benefit for beings is thought to warrant it. In par-

ticular, with its increasing emphasis upon *karunā* [compassion] the ethos comes to resemble the Christian ethic of agapism. (Keown, 1992:185)

Keown goes on (185-191) to present Joseph Fletcher's view of "Situation Ethics" which he perceptively calls "Agapistic Act-Utilitarianism." The "Mahā-yāna-*upāya*" view is that of the great Bodhisattvas who, like the Roshi who teaches the samurai about heaven and hell, act compassionately sometimes in disregard of general precepts; and, this does seem to mirror Fletcher's view that the only principle or value that the Christian needs to be guided by is that "unconditioned love" that God has for us.

In *Utilitarianism*, J. S. Mill famously claims:

As between his own happiness and that of others, utilitarianism requires him to be as strictly impartial as a disinterested and benevolent spectator. In the golden rule of Jesus of Nazareth, we read the complete spirit of the ethics of utility. 'To do as you would be done by,' and 'to love your neighbor as yourself,' constitute the ideal of perfection of utilitarian morality. (Mill, 1979:16-17)

Now, it is true that utilitarianism, in advocating the maximization of happiness and the minimization of suffering, does count all beings equally in light of (or in proportion to) their presumed capacities to experience happiness and suffering. Whereas traditionally utilitarianism holds that the moral value of an act is determined solely by the net utility of its consequences, clearly the virtue of the agent should be judged by the purity of intent in bringing about those consequences; and, if the agent is acting out of love, as commanded by God, then that is different than if he were acting out of purely self-interested motives. What Fletcher's Situation Ethics advocates is the combination of virtuous motivation with utilitarian outcomes, thus the rubric, "Agapistic Act Utilitarianism."

What is revealing is to consider Fletcher's proposition, "Love and Justice are the same, for justice is love distributed, nothing else." (Fletcher, 1966:86, emphasis deleted) Here, to love others is to will for them as much net good (benefit, happiness) over bad (harm, suffering) as possible; to seek justice is, in treating all equally, to seek the greatest possible distribution of love, i.e., the greatest net utility. So, acting out of a motive of "love," for Fletcher, does not alter one iota the act that one should be prepared to do as recommended by any act-utilitarian, regardless of agent-motivation. Regarding Noddings' battered-wife from an Agapist Act-Utilitarian perspective, and assuming that the abusing husband's life has no greater utility value than anyone else's, then, out of love "for all concerned," aggregately, the wife ought to kill her husband. But, surely this stands "Christian ethics" on its head, for how is killing someone, in this circumstance, doing unto another as one would want to be done unto?

There is an even more fundamental problem with an act-utilitarian approach to decision-making and it has to do with what has *moral* value. Act-utilitarians generally hold: (a) what is desire-satisfying has positive value (is "good") and what is desire-frustrating has negative value (is "evil"); (b) the amount of such value is dependent upon the degree of desirability (desire-satisfaction) or non-desirability, respectively; and (c) to do what is "right," in any given circumstance is to maximize "good" and/or minimize "evil," so construed. It is well known that this approach easily runs into putative counter-examples: fulfilling the sexual desires of many may "outweigh" the painful consequences of sexually exploiting someone who "volunteers" her sexual favors for a goal that is falsely promised; fulfilling the desires of many for vengeance and retaliation may outweigh the terrible beating inflicted on a suspected rapist; and so on. In these kinds of cases, the clear harm done to the "victim" is weighed against the purported "benefits" to those inflicting harm. Moreover, one may ask, is happiness fundamentally a matter of "desire-satisfaction?" Are the sexual predators and avengers really "better off" for having their (malicious) desires satisfied? How is one's well being (happiness) related to desire-satisfaction? Well, if one is in a state of deprivation of what one *needs*, then one is suffering; and, in so far as one fulfills desires for what one needs, then, it seems, one is treating oneself compassionately. On this view, what is desired-as-needed is to be relieved of deprivation. So, happiness or well-being is not an "added value" to one's life, but rather just is one's enjoying a natural, non-deprived state of being. Richard Taylor expresses the point (made by Schopenhauer) this way: "Happiness...consists in the absence of misery and torment, and a happy life, to the extent that it is possible, is nothing more than a life relatively free from suffering." (Taylor, 1985:167) Obviously, the satisfaction of desires for recreational sex and revenge are not so needed; hence satisfying such desires has no moral value and cannot be "weighed" morally against causing beings harm.

Recall that we noted (Ch III.2) that, for Schopenhauer, "The concepts *wrong* and *right* are synonymous with doing harm and not doing harm, and to the latter belongs also the warding off of injury." (Schopenhauer, 1995:154) From this *moral* point of view, the *evil* that is to be avoided is the *causing* of "harm" or "injury" and the *good* to be pursued is the *prevention* of harm or injury. Any *ethical* maximization principle should seek, then, to maximize what is *morally* good and to minimize what is *morally* evil, rather than to maximize what is judged to be "good" on the basis of "desire-satisfactions." Indeed, often practical choice presents us with options between doing the "prudentially-advantageous" action, all things considered, and doing the "morally preferred" action, all things considered. Prudential and moral values are not all commensurable—there is no general "standard" by which they can be measured against each other.[5]

A critical difference between utilitarian ethics and compassion ethics is that the most basic principle of utilitarianism is to "maximize" what it takes to be of value, whereas compassion ethics, like Kantian ethics, gives priority to the intentionality of acting according to one's principles or precepts. In Chapter III.3, we eschewed the notion that compassionate intentionality is subject to a standard of distributive justice; if one is acting to impartially relieve others' sufferings, that is sufficient for one's doing what is morally right regardless of how one's efforts are distributed over the needy. So too, one does what is morally right if one is fulfilling one's compassionate intentionality, regardless of whether one also is maximizing the value of one's efforts, e g , human welfare generally. What gives moral value to one's behavior is the compassionate intentionality of not harming others but rather relieving their sufferings. Furthermore, it hardly makes sense to think that one should be maximizing one's "compassionate intentionality," although, it does make sense for one to aim to be skillful in relieving beings from their sufferings; but whether such skillfulness might result in "the greatest happiness of the greatest number" is not an issue that even arises. When Samuel Oliner rescued the German pilot or when the Good Samaritan came to the aid of the battered traveler, what "foreseeable consequences" beyond the immediacy of their care are relevant to their acting compassionately?

In conclusion, Buddhist-oriented precepts for avoiding doing evil may be practiced as authentic expressions of "Golden Rule" reasoning, of what it means to "love one's neighbor as oneself" or to "act compassionately." Furthermore, how these precepts are grounded and how they operate differ from explanations for similar looking rules provided by Western normative theories. Important issues nevertheless remain regarding the nature of "well-being" and what has "moral value." In Chapter V, we will explore the role of "virtue" in an ethics of compassion in contrast with the relationship between virtue and "well-being" in Aristotle as well as the Buddhist claim that it is precisely one's generalized will for desire-satisfaction and pain-avoidance that lies at the heart of one's lack of well-being, of one's continued suffering.

NOTES

1. In the Mahāyāna Buddhist tradition, there are commonly thought to be five basic precepts of right action. The precepts have a positive ("do good") and a negative ("avoid doing evil") side and are vows one takes as "mindfulness trainings." (See, e.g., Thich Nhat Hanh, 1992:81-97) Following Loori (1996:82-95), they may be expressed as:

I vow to affirm life and to refrain from the taking of life
I vow to be generous and to refrain from taking what is not given
I vow to honor the body and to refrain from sexual misconduct
I vow to manifest truth and to refrain from verbal transgressions
I vow to proceed clearly and to refrain from harmful consumption

The refraining "proscriptions" may be considered as "precepts of obligation" (to avoid doing evil) and may be derived from (5), whereas the "positive" prescriptions may be understood as "precepts of aspiration" (to do good) and may be derived from (5a). In the Buddhist literature, the five refraining precepts discussed in this volume are commonly referred to as constituting "right action;" here "right action" simply is not engaging in "wrong action" that causes injury or suffering. In this tradition, principle (5a) is subordinate to principle (5); one is not to "do good" in ways that cause serious suffering. In fact, on the Buddhist view, as well as in other Eastern traditions, "good" simply is the absence of suffering; beings who are free from suffering are in natural states of well-being. At any rate, a discussion of the precepts of aspiration, as well as of the role of the virtues in relation to the cultivation of compassion, must await Chapter V.

2. Buddhism shares the view that death is *per se* a great suffering and is separate from whatever suffering one may experience in the course of dying. From the Buddhist perspective, then, any intentional death causes unnecessary suffering; in particular, the suffering of death is greater than, and hence cannot be warranted by, the suffering that one experiences in dying. It should not be thought that in order for death to be a suffering that it must be "experienced." In the western tradition, the state's execution of a murderer is thought by retributivists to rectify that scale of justice by making the criminal suffer the same (degree of) "harm" as the murderer caused his victim; this would occur even if the victim and/or the criminal were to die painlessly (or unknowingly).

3. Classical Christian moral theology does not find intentional killing in self-defense to be justifiable, although it may be excusable from human blame. A text from St. Bonaventure's *Collations on the Ten Commandments* (VI.9) reads:

> If a murder takes place by reason of necessity, this can happen in two ways: either by a necessity that can be avoided or by a necessity that cannot be avoided. A necessity that can be avoided is if I am able to circumvent the situation, and I do not, because of shame or some other reason. In this instance a person is excused from such but not all, because it would be better to shun the situation. A necessity that cannot be avoided is when a person as an individual kills another, not for the sake of revenge, but for the sake of self-preservation; not out of cruelty, but so that he might prevent the other from [killing] him; and if this [killing] is done with the restraint of self-preservation, then that which is not allowed to a perfect person,* is allowed to an imperfect person (as Augustine says in *Libero Arbitrio*), and he is excused from all and from such.

> *The perfect person "would turn the other cheek" and allow himself to be killed (*Matthew* 5:39, *Luke* 6:29)—editor's note
>
>   St. Bonaventure, 1995:87-88

Writing in the same period as Bonaventure, Thomas Aquinas also refused to justify one's *intentionally* killing another in self defense. (*ST*, II-II, Q. 64, Art. 7)

4. Indeed, among Buddhists, many take a "Kantian" approach to the precepts and consider at least the first four to be applicable for all moral agents in all circumstances. (See, e.g., Keown, 1992:232)

5. Such cases are vital to explain "moral weakness" and "free will." See for example Reilly (1977a) and Kane (1999), whose analyses of "dual rational control" of one's conduct presume the incommensurability of these sets of goods or values. This matter is discussed in detail in Ch. VI, Sections 2-3 below.

Chapter V
Virtues and Moral Aspiration

Those of highest benevolence act, but without ulterior motives.

The Sage has no heart of his own;
He uses the heart of the people as his heart.

Laozi, Tao Tê Ching, 38 & 49

So far, we have discussed precepts of right action in light of the principle of duty: one ought not to cause other beings to suffer unnecessarily. We have seen that there is a "rational ground" of this principle which itself serves as a rational basis of the precepts. We have noted, furthermore, that this ground is one's human nature: the will to live, to prosper and to avoid unnecessary suffering as well as the capacities to see in other living beings a similar nature and to wish for other beings what we wish for ourselves.

Even though compassion is the basis of right action, that is, of not causing harm to others but rather relieving others from harm, it still might appear that the picture of the moral life so far drawn is overly "intellectual" and does not integrate sufficiently the "emotional" dimensions of human nature. In this chapter, we will examine the significance of "vices" and "virtues" in light of the task of moral development. Vices are those dispositional states or attitudes rooted in narrow self-centeredness that motivate one to act independently of, and, hence, often against, the (ground of the) precepts of not causing harm. The virtues, on the other hand, are dispositional states or attitudes that enable one to transcend narrow self-centeredness and, hence, to direct oneself in accordance with the (ground of the) precepts. To "act virtuously" and to "act on principle" are opposite sides of the same coin; however, to be fully virtuous is to be effortlessly responsive to the requirements of the situation one is in without any self-regarding motive.

73

This chapter is divided into four sections. The first section discusses the dominant Western view of virtue having its roots in Homeric Greek culture and in the philosophy of Plato and Aristotle. To generalize, on the Greek view virtue (*arête*) empowers one to actualize one's human potentials within the circumstances of one's life; living virtuously enables one to flourish within the community. The second section provides a contrasting view of virtue from the tradition of Mahāyāna Buddhism; here the practices of certain virtues (*paramitas*) have as their result one's transcendence of the "self" which, in the Greek tradition, one seeks to actualize. The *paramitas* are connected with the "positive" sides of the precepts of right action which form what I call "responsibilities of moral aspiration" and apply to three dimensions of right-living: right livelihood, right citizenship and right subsistence. The third section explores what the "transcendence of self-centeredness" (or "selflessness") means and why it does not entail "desirelessness." I close with an appendix that explains why it is not the case that the Buddha's teachings on the "liberation from suffering" require one to attain a state of "desirelessness" (as is commonly thought).

1. Arête

Following A.W.H. Adkins (1960) and Alasdair MacIntyre (1966), one may think of the virtues of Homeric society as forming two classes: the "competitive virtues" that contribute to "success" in the domains of war, politics and economics and the "cooperative virtues" that contribute to harmonious and effective relations in the everyday life of the community. Examples of the former are those we might associate with a military hero, a political statesman or an industry leader: vision, ambition, practical intelligence (in strategic and tactical planning and execution), perseverance, courage and public esteem; all this results in a person of unexcelled position or power, an *agathos* or "great man." Examples of the latter are honesty, fair-mindedness, generosity, kindness, and so on; these mark the morally decent person.

In Homeric Greece, the cooperative virtues or values were subordinated to the competitive virtues or values should the two come into conflict; in short, "might" or "success" makes right. There was no obligation for an *agathos* to be honest or fair-minded as long as he maintains his position; he should be honest and fair-minded in so far as being so would contribute to his overall aims and position; but, if it were beneficial (in the long run) to act dishonestly or unfairly, which is to say, "unjustly" in his treatment of others, then he need not hesitate to do so. (Adkins, 1960:48-57)

It is against this background that Socrates, Plato and Aristotle fashioned their views on living virtuously. Plato's Socrates held a view that commentators still call a "paradox," namely that no one does injustice or wrong willingly; this view obviously would be thought absurd by anyone who believes that Homeric heroes are paradigms of what it means to be *agathoi*. Nevertheless, Plato makes his case in the *Gorgias* and the structure of his argument is worth considering.[1]

Assume:

(1) A fact of human nature: no one wants to be unhappy; rather,

(2) Everyone wants to be happy and so wills what is good (or best) or more beneficial for oneself. (468c)

From which we may derive:

(3) The doctrine of psychological egoism: all actions are pursued for what the agent considers to be, on balance, good, i.e., the most beneficial or least harmful results for himself. (467d-68d)

A corollary of which is:

(4) The prudential paradox: no one willingly pursues evil, i.e., the more harmful or less beneficial. (468c-d)

If we now add:

(5) The principle of justice: it is always better (more beneficial) to do justice than injustice. (470c, in light of 469b, 470e, 474d)

We may conclude:

(6) The moral paradox: no one does injustice (or wrong) willingly, but all who do injustice (or wrong) do so involuntarily. (509e)

Even though Socrates characterizes injustice as an "evil condition of the soul" (477b), the arguments against Polus and Callicles indicate that the "harm" it produces is of the prudential sort which is commonly dread; the harm not being in one's soul but rather in one's life in consequence of one's unjust soul or character. Like Book IX of *The Republic*, the *Gorgias* presents the view that unjust tyrants or extreme wrong-doers, out of fear and repercussion, fail to attain what they will, namely happiness. (468d) To the contrary, as a consequence of their injustice, they might find themselves lonely, both untrusted and untrusting, and without friends (cf. 510b-e), or suffering ostracism, banishment, or perhaps untimely death (516d), but certainly eternal punishment (525c-e). In brief, injustice is the greatest of evils, on Plato's view, because it does not allow its possessor to enjoy the satisfying, integrated life within a community, but, rather, it multiplies the possibilities of one's being harmed in return. To choose injustice or wrongdoing risks the result of becoming, perhaps through habituation, an unjust person, who, being a fearful slave of his own actions, can look forward to the most wretched of futures.[2]

Although Aristotle's treatment of virtue has a quite different orientation from Plato's, there are some significant areas of conceptual overlap. For Aristotle, virtues are powers for rationally managing emotions so as to enable one to live a life most "satisfying," "successful," "flourishing" or "happy." Aristotle writes: "...it is thought to be a mark of a man of practical wisdom to be able to deliberate well about what is good and expedient for himself, not in some particular respect . . . but about what sorts of things conduce to the good life in general." (*Nic. Eth.*:1140a25-28) In short, "Aristotle's claim then is that the best man is the man who exercises his rational capacities to their fullest to *gain for himself the best life possible*." (Wilkes, 1980:354)

Running through the Homeric, Platonic and Aristotelian views discussed above is the notion that "virtues" are excellences of character that enable one to be successful in achieving what is good or best for oneself; moreover, with the exception of

Socrates and Plato, doing so consists in living a life of attainment within the community and is normally accompanied by the respect if not esteem of one's fellows. Even the practice of justice, as with the cooperative virtues generally, is tied to the honorable regard of one's fellows—one benefits immensely from the reputation of being honest, trustworthy, fair, and loyal in one's dealings with friends and acquaintances. To fail to act "virtuously" results in failure to gain important goods for oneself; as a consequence, one's behavior is seen by others as being "shameful" and "weak." A common explanation of such failure is that one's behavior was under the influence of a "vice," that is, an improper habituation of an emotion such as anger, fear, greed, hate, lust, envy, and so on, which motivates one to act in ways counter to one's best interests.

Emotions are like "feeling states" that one may be in control of or be controlled by. Aristotle's well known view is that each virtue is a "mean" relative to two ways of failing to properly control one's emotion—either due to its excess or to its deficiency. So, for example, if one gets too angry, too readily, and not always with the proper persons for appropriate reasons, the behavior that results likely will be inappropriate and manifest too much emotion and too little reason (rational control). At the same time, one who is deficient in experiencing and/or expressing an emotion is also blameworthy.

> For those who are not angry at the things they should be angry at are thought to be fools, and so are those who are not angry in the right way, at the right time, or with the right persons; for such a man is thought not to feel things nor to be pained by them, and, since he does not get angry, he is thought unlikely to defend himself; and to endure being insulted and put up with insult to one's friends is slavish. (*Nic. Eth.*, 1126a4-8)

The ill-tempered person may get angry too quickly, or get too angry when he gets angry, or stay angry too long, or express his anger violently in which cases the vices of hot-temperedness, bad-temperedness, bitterness and violence are exhibited respectively. (Cf. Hutchinson, 1995:219) People exhibiting such vices typically suffer as a result. To avoid self-defeating conduct, one must practice the virtues—settled habits of character that express themselves in the correct emotional response to the situation at hand. (Hutchinson, 1995:213) The good-tempered person manages to get angry in the appropriate circumstance, in an appropriate manner, with respect to an appropriate object; often such "well controlled" anger expresses a second virtue—for instance, justice, as in the case where one gets angry at a perpetrator of injustice and is thereby moved to act constructively to rectify the injustice and/or bring about reconciliation between the perpetrator and the victim of the injustice. It is important to note Aristotelian virtues presume societal "standards" and that it is characteristic of Aristotle to take the "common" and "reasonable" view to establish such standards, e.g., in this case for what kinds of insults one should not endure but rather "defend" oneself (or friends) against. This is an important point, since, as Martha Nussbaum (2001:159-61) has shown, the "appropriateness" of anger ranges widely across cultures.

For Aristotle, virtues and vices are states of character and states of character are habits or dispositions which normally result from processes of habituation in one's youth.

> Thus, in one word, states of character arise out of like activities. This is why the activities we exhibit must be of a certain kind; it is because states of character correspond to the differences between these. It makes no small difference, then, whether we form habits of one kind or another from our very youth; it makes a very great difference, or rather *all* the difference. (*Nic. Eth.*, 1103b20-25)

Socialization accounts for the virtues that one develops and what they mean. What it means to be generous or courageous or just is reflected in the kinds of acts that one's society deems "generous," "courageous," and "just;" and it is by performing acts of these kinds that, by habituation, one develops a virtuous character. As we have seen, the underlying presumption is that the virtues make possible one's flourishing relative to the norms of society. To do what is socially appropriate or commendable is not necessarily to do, as Kant saw, what has moral value. Indeed, for a Kantian the cultivation of the virtues "always means the reproduction of a certain kind of human personality that was well adjusted to society based on unenlightened traditions, inequalities, forms of oppression—in short, on the radical propensity to evil that belongs to our nature as social beings." (Wood, 2008:157)

Interestingly, Aristotle also gave voice to the quite different view that the end of the good life is *contemplation*; that one should lead a life dominated by theoretical wisdom rather than practical wisdom. "Self-realization" here involves identifying with the divine nature; and, it would seem, this requires relinquishing, rather than fulfilling or realizing, the "self" of social aspiration.[3] In this light, it would be quite appropriate to think of the "beatitudes" that Jesus preached as virtues--albeit for achieving oneness with God rather than earthly "success" or "fulfillment" (Cf. Forest, 20). Nevertheless, the dominant view of the virtues in Western philosophy is that they serve the purpose of living successfully in this life. In the Buddhist tradition, the "householder" is encouraged to practice a range of virtues similar to what Aristotle would prescribe for the political man. (Saddhatissa, 1977, Ch. 6-7) However, for the Buddhist the ultimate aim of one's life is "liberation" from the everyday world of *samsara* (cyclic, suffering existence) and the distinctive virtues of Buddhist practice are called "*paramitas*," or "transcendental perfections," that is, ways of transcending self-centeredness, ways of becoming "selfless," of "extinguishing self" and attaining "nirvana." The selfless person acts to benefit all beings rather than to attain "success" or to "flourish" in ways defined by social approbation and attainment.

2. The *Paramitas* and Universal Responsibility

Jesus is recorded to have said:

> You have heard that it was said to the men of old, 'You shall not kill; and whoever
> kills shall be subject to punishment.' But, I say to you that every one who is angry
> with his brother shall be liable to judgment. . . . You have heard that it was said,
> 'You shall not commit adultery.' But I say to you that every one who looks at a
> woman lustfully has already committed adultery with her in his heart. (*Matthew*,
> 5:21-22, 27-28)

Motivating non-virtuous, intentional conduct is either some form of hostility or some
form of covetousness; both are rooted in ignorance, in a false sense of "self" as an
independent, self-subsisting being. In discussing the First Precept, Saddhatissa
(1977:62-70) recounts ten methods to subdue anger by "loving-kindness" meditative
practices so to pacify if not eliminate one's motivation to take the life of another.
The path to virtue is not to be subject to the "irrational emotions" but to "uproot"
them if possible; and, since such emotions are deeply embedded in a "false" sense of
self-identity, what must be overcome is precisely a centeredness on such a sense of
"self;" if possible, one should "transcend" the ego-self altogether.

At this point, one might raise this question: how is it possible for a person to
transcend his or her ego and be(come) compassionate? Would not any motive to do
so be an expression of ego itself? Certainly, one's practice should not be motivated
by the "eight ordinary concerns:" gain or loss, pleasure or pain, praise or blame,
honor (fame) or shame (infamy), for all these are rooted in ego. On the other hand, if
one's motive is not self-centered, but, say, (the desire for) the happiness of all sentient beings or (the desire) to be one with God, then one may engage in practices that
do not serve egoistic self-interest. True, one may still have self-interests; but one can
meaningfully take on the task of reducing the strength and scope of their influence,
to continue to whittle away at them, little by little, until self-interest disappears altogether. One's egoistic self-interests dissipate as one's ego-identity dissolves, when
one no longer identifies oneself as separate and independent of others. When one
attains wisdom, the integration of all the *paramitas*, one sees the inter-dependent
origination or inter-being of self and phenomena and one embodies compassion.

Chogyam Trungpa Rinpoche introduces the *paramitas* as the path of the *bodhi-*
sattva, of one "who is brave enough to walk on the path . . . of the awakened ones."

> They are: transcendental generosity, discipline, patience, energy, meditation, and
> knowledge (*prajna*). These virtues are called the six *paramitas*, because *param*
> means "other side" or "shore," "other side of the river," and *ita* means "arrived."
> *Paramita* means "arriving at the other side or shore," which indicates that the activi-
> ties of the bodhisattva must have the vision, the understanding which transcends the
> centralized notions of ego. The bodhisattva is not trying to be good or kind, but he is
> spontaneously compassionate. (Trungpa, 1993:170)

From one point of view, the *paramitas* cover the entire "Noble Eightfold Path" of
wisdom (*prajna*), morality (*sila*) and meditation; moreover, they are interdependent
in practice. "Understanding" them fully can take a lifetime. Nonetheless, it will
prove instructive to summarize the *paramitas* and then to comment on them generally.[4]

Generosity is "communication," says Trungpa, that is, "radiation and receiving and exchange" rather than simply giving; it transcends irritations and difference; it is a willingness to give without pious motive, to be open without judgment, evaluation, preference. Fundamentally, it is the practice of love, of just simply doing what is required at any moment in any situation, not being afraid to receive anything. What do we have to offer, to give? Our true presence, our stability, our freedom, our freshness, our peace, our space, our understanding, says Thich Nhat Hanh.

Discipline (*sila*) covers the entire range of the precepts of not causing harm, of "right conduct." The bodhisattva acts according to openness, not premeditatively, not distinguishing between this and that but with pure "equanimity." Like an elephant, walking slowly, surely, each step is solid, definite.

Patience is an inclusiveness that is rooted in never expecting anything; not expecting, one is never impatient (angry, perturbed, judgmental). Being always aware of the space between the situation and oneself, the bodhisattva is never surprised or disturbed, but just flows with the situation.

Energy is diligence rooted in the abundant joy one experiences in the creative patterns of life; the bodhisattva sees situations from a panoramic point of view, never tires of working with life, never dwells in a dull moment.

Meditation ("Zen") is being one with the present moment, the present situation; the bodhisattva's action is always meditation and her meditation is always action. Meditation combines "calm-abiding" with insight, in "looking deeply" one sees that phenomena and self are not independent, separated realities, but are interdependent, mutually arising.

Knowledge (*prajna*, wisdom), says Trungpa, is twofold: the *prajna* of knowing cuts through conflicting emotions; the *prajna* of seeing reveals situations as they truly are. There is no distinguishing between this and that for the bodhisattva. Thich Nhat Hanh calls *prajna paramita* "the wisdom of non-discrimination."

> If you look deeply into the person you love, you'll be able to understand her suffering, her difficulties, and also her deepest aspirations. And out of that understanding, real love will be possible. When someone is able to understand us, we feel very happy. If we can offer understanding to someone, that is true love. The one who receives our understanding will bloom like a flower, and we will be rewarded at the same time. Understanding is the fruit of the practice...Looking deeply into any object, understanding will flower. (Hanh, 1998:211)

Whereas understanding is the fruit of meditation, we might say that compassion is the fruit, the result, of understanding. To illustrate the inter-penetration of the *paramitas*, consider this episode related by Thich Nhat Hanh in *Touching Peace*.

> One boy who practices at Plum Village told me this story. When he was eleven, he was very angry at his father. Every time he fell down and hurt himself, his father would get angry and shout at him. The boy vowed that when he grew up, he would be different. But a few years ago, his little sister was playing with other children and fell off a swing and scraped her knee. It was bleeding and the boy became very angry. He wanted to shout at her, "How stupid! Why did you do that?" But he caught

himself. Because he had been practicing mindfulness [meditation], he knew how to recognize anger as anger, and he did not act on it.

A number of adults who were present were taking good care of his sister, washing her wound and putting a bandage on it, so he walked away slowly and practiced looking deeply. Suddenly he saw that he was exactly like his father, and he recognized that if he did do something about his anger, he would transmit it to his children. It was a remarkable insight for an eleven-year-old boy. At the same time, he saw that his father may have been a victim just like him. The seeds of his father's anger might have been transmitted by his grandparents. Because of the practice of looking deeply in mindfulness, he was able to transform his anger into insight. Then he went to his father, and told him that because he now understood him, he was able to really love him. (Hanh, 1992:31-32)

The boy's practice of the *paramitas*, while not perfected, is illustrative in its concreteness of their inter-connectedness. That the boy did not act out of anger, displayed discipline in conforming to the precepts of right-conduct; that he continued to "look deeply" reflects diligence in practicing mindfulness (meditation); and, as a result of his looking deeply, he gained an understanding of the interdependent-origination of anger and of the "sameness" of himself and his father; and from this understanding, an expression of love generously manifested.

The attitudes of "openness," "spaciousness," and "being non-judgmental" are interrelated fruits of meditative practice. Often, "openness" (or "emptiness") is equated with "compassion." (Guenther, 1975) What such openness involves is that one not identify anything as "me"/"mine" or "not me"/"not mine;" which is to say, "there is no distinguishing between this and that." This is what uproots desire (that something be mine) and hatred (for what is not me or mine), the wellsprings of non-virtuous or harmful conduct. The practice of generosity, of not identifying anything as exclusively "mine" but making everything available to those in need, is the main antidote to greed, self-centered desire; and it is the practice of patience, of not allowing expectations or "prejudgments" to define one's attitudes to other beings or to the situations one is in, that is, the main antidote for hostility in its various forms (e.g., non-acceptance, irritation, impatience, criticism, anger, dislike, and hatred). The effective practice of generosity and patience, however, require the cultivation of the other virtues as well.

One should aspire to be compassionate or to act compassionately in whatever situation one finds oneself. In light of this, the "precepts" take on added significance and meaning. While our previous analysis looked at precepts in light of the principle of duty not to cause suffering, there are corresponding precepts to protect/relieve beings from suffering. While the "main" practice in abiding in the precepts involves not causing suffering, each precept has a positive side as well. Roshi Loorie (84-93) presents the precepts this way: (1) Affirm Life. Do not kill. (2) Be giving. Do not steal. (3) Honor the body. Do not misuse sexuality. (4) Manifest truth. Do not lie. (5) Proceed clearly. Do not cloud the mind. The positive prescriptions I call "responsibilities of aspiration;" they call upon us to be as mindful, as compassionate, as possible. Since, these positive "precepts" cannot be expressed as determinate rules of obligation, they are better understood as "responsibilities" or "mindfulness trainings" in the manner articulated by Thich Nhat Hanh.

Affirm Life

Aware of the suffering caused by the destruction of life, I am committed to cultivating compassion and learning ways to protect the lives of people, animals, plants, and minerals. I am determined not to kill, not to let others kill, and not to support any act of killing in the world, in my thinking, and in my way of life. (Hanh, 1992:82)

Be Giving

Aware of the suffering caused by exploitation, social injustice, stealing and oppression, I am committed to cultivating loving kindness and learning ways to work for the well being of people, animals, plants, and minerals. I will practice generosity by sharing my time, energy, and material resources with those who are in real need. I am determined not to steal and not to possess anything that should belong to others. I will respect the property of others, but I will prevent others from profiting from human suffering or the suffering of other species on Earth. (Hanh, 1992:83)

Honor the Body

Aware of the suffering caused by sexual misconduct, I am committed to cultivating responsibility and learning ways to protect the safety and integrity of individuals, couples, families, and society. I am determined not to engage in sexual relations without love and long-term commitment. To preserve the happiness of myself and others, I am determined to respect the commitments of others. I will do everything in my power to protect children from sexual abuse and to prevent couples and families from being broken by sexual misconduct. (Hanh, 1992:84-85)

Manifest Truth

Aware of the suffering caused by unmindful speech and the inability to listen to others, I am committed to cultivating loving speech and deep listening in order to bring joy and happiness to others and relieve others of their suffering. Knowing that words can create happiness or suffering, I am determined to Speak truthfully, with words that inspire self-confidence, joy, and hope. I will not spread news that I do not know to be certain and will not criticize or condemn things of which I am not sure. I will refrain from uttering words that can cause division or discord, or that can cause the family or community to break. I am determined to make all efforts to reconcile and resolve all conflicts, however small. (Hanh, 1992:87)

Proceed Clearly

Aware of the suffering caused by unmindful consumption, I am committed to cultivating good health, both physical and mental, for myself, my family, and my society by practicing mindful eating, drinking, and consuming. I will ingest only items that preserve peace, well being, and joy in my body, in my consciousness, and in the collective body of my family and society. I am determined not to use alcohol or any other intoxicant or to ingest foods or other items, such as certain TV programs, magazines, books, films, and conversations. I am aware that to damage my body or my consciousness with these poisons is to betray my ancestors, my parents, my society, and future generations. I will work to trans-form violence, fear, anger, confusion in myself, and in society by practicing a diet for myself and for society. I understand that a proper diet is crucial for self-transformation and for the transformation of society. (Hanh, 1992:89)

By grounding one's "commitments" and "determinations" in one's own awareness of the causes of suffering, as does Thich Nhat Hanh, one fashions an "inalienable, continuously developing, and self orienting ethic," to borrow Schweitzer's
phrase. Such an ethic of first-person precepts expresses one's mindfulness; as one's
mindfulness matures and deepens, one's commitments and determinations broaden
and sharpen. What is central is the intention to act compassionately in whatever
situation one is in. One's skillfulness resides in the effective utilization of available
resources to relieve, as much as possible, the suffering of others. Clearly, this presumes that one has practiced and developed the virtues of generosity, patience, diligence, discipline, mindfulness and wisdom. On the view presented here, acting appropriately with compassionate intention to do what one can is to fulfill one's moral
responsibility in that moment or situation.

For most of the ancient Greek thinkers, the practice of virtue was defined by,
and confined to, the community/culture in which one lives. At least since the
Enlightenment, however, Western moral philosophy has presumed the global reach
of one's moral concern. The Dalai Lama expresses the point this way:

> To develop a sense of universal responsibility—of the universal dimension of our
> every act and of the equal right of all others to happiness and not to suffer—is to de-
> velop an attitude of mind whereby, when we see an opportunity to benefit others, we
> take it in preference to merely looking out after our narrow interests. But though, of
> course, we care about what is beyond our scope, we accept it as part of nature and
> concern ourselves with doing what we can. (Dalai Lama, 1999:162-163)

Moral precepts do not hold only for particular persons or groups of persons at particular times or in particular places, but rather they extend to all beings everywhere at
any time; in their universal dimension they should be practiced within the domains of
livelihood, citizenship and consumption.

Right Livelihood

We have noted that the "positive" responsibilities one has to those whom one is in
close relation with, e.g., family and friends, should be fulfilled within the parameters
of one's "negative" duties to not cause harm to others. A householder who has responsibilities to raise and educate children as well as to contribute to the common
good, i.e., to help establish/maintain adequate schools, healthcare facilities, welfare
services, public utilities and sanitation, and so on, needs to have the means sufficient
to do so. It is not, then, primarily for one's own comfort and pleasure that one needs
to acquire income or perhaps wealth. One's efforts at earning income or wealth are
warranted by the good that results, presuming that they do not involve intentional
violations of the precepts of right action. Traditionally, refraining from occupations
that *require or necessarily involve* violations of the precepts of right action is "right
livelihood;" such occupations include: trade in weapons, human beings, flesh, intoxicants, and poison. (Saddhatissa, 1977:107; *Anguttaranikaya*, III, 208) So, for example, being a butcher would be in violation of right livelihood since it involves the

slaughter of animals. Interestingly, participating in some of the other trades mentioned may not require one to directly violate a precept, but it clearly contributes to (abets) others who do so; trading in intoxicants (e.g., heroin) or poisons (e.g., for the euthanasia of animals at "shelters" or insecticides for lawn beautification) in situations where those purchasing them would willingly permit them to cause suffering unnecessarily would mean that one is willing to earn his or her livelihood at the expense of the suffering of others. Indeed, a trader or distributor of intoxicants or poisons might wish for their increased consumption in order for his or her business to grow. If we hold that one intends, or shares in the responsibility for, the suffering that results naturally (predictably) from one's intentional actions, then the range of "right livelihood" narrows considerably.

The range narrows considerably more if one looks at "right livelihood" not simply as "not causing suffering" (even indirectly) but as "protecting/relieving beings from suffering" for this would call into question the propriety of work that has little or no effect on the weal as well as on the woe of one's fellow beings. Moreover, distinct from the suffering and benefit that mark the effects of one's work, there is also the suffering and benefit that resides in (the nature of) one's work or in one's work in a given environment. For instance, does one's work allow one to express oneself creatively or spiritually? Is it work that one is able to do, and permitted to do, with full awareness and care? What opportunities (or obstacles) does the workplace present for being in communion with others and for practicing the virtues, especially "right speech," while at work?

One's work should not impede, but rather it should contribute to, one's progressively becoming a compassionate being. In first-world nations, given the freedom of choice one has in preparing for and selecting a career as well as a work environment, one incurs a greater degree of responsibility to practice "right livelihood." Roger Pritchard asserts:

> Right livelihood demands that you take responsibility for making your work meaningful. Good work is dignified. It develops your faculties and serves your community. It is a central human activity. Work, in this view:
> makes you honest with yourself
> requires that you develop your faculties and skills
> empowers you to do what you are really good at and love to do
> connects you in a compassionate way with the outside world
> supports the philosophy of non-destructiveness and sustainability
> integrates work with personal life and community. (Pritchard, 1994: 212)

Of course, it is not that "work" should "do" these things for us, but that "in work" we might accomplish these things. Often we have to "work with our work" to actualize its potential benefits. We even might have to "work" at getting really good at what we do for work or at learning to like if not love our work; or, we might have to "work" at integrating our work with our home life and our moral priorities.

Precisely because right livelihood, as with practicing the precepts generally, is a collective matter, to live mindfully involves one's addressing the issues posed by the interrelatedness of our ways of life, by whatever suffering occurs in consequence of

our economic, social, and political practice. Social roles in and of themselves generally do not ground moral responsibilities. One always might inquire, "Given that
such-and-such role ("husband," "physician," "corporate officer," and so on) requires
that I do so-and-so, ought I to assume (or remain in) that role? It is in this context
that we share a "universal responsibility" to do what we can, given our resources and
circumstances, to help others. Furthermore, just as our (families') economic interests
must be pursued in a manner consistent with our moral responsibilities, so should our
commitments as a state-citizen be undertaken in a manner consistent with our global
responsibilities to all those beings who share our planet and may be affected by our
actions and by our example.

Right Citizenship

Surely one owes much to one's state, especially if it is justly ordered, protects individuals from suffering and promotes the common good. Both out of gratitude and a
sense of fair play, one should do one's civic duty—uphold just laws, pay a fair share
of taxes, vote if eligible, and otherwise participate in the political life of the community. Society can function harmoniously to the extent that its citizens are honest,
moral, generous, and tolerant in their dealings with one another; in addition, families
should be as self-reliant as possible, manifesting energy, industriousness, and skillfulness in right livelihood; and people should engage in voluntary service that contributes to the happiness of others as well as support public programs serving the
common good in such areas as education, healthcare, and employment.

   The legitimate authority of the state, however, does not extend to policies and
practices that involve intentional violations of precepts of duty--especially the killing
and exploitation of human beings. The tendency in classical Greek and Roman culture was to subordinate conscience and "personal morality" to the laws and interests
of the state.[5] Since Locke and Rousseau, however, a broadly accepted underlying
assumption in political philosophy has been that one's moral identity is independent
of one's status as "citizen." What it means to be a "citizen" in the modern age appears to be full "enfranchisement" under the laws of a state or municipality on the
one hand, and a general obligation to obey the laws and to support their constitu-
tional authority on the other hand. On the Lockean model of the Social Contract,
individuals in the state of nature recognize basic moral principles and enjoy a communal life, though one fraught with danger and uncertainty. To better assure their
"natural" rights to life, liberty and property, it indeed would be rational for such individuals to come together to establish a body politic wherein each gives up his or
her right to "punish" those who violate one's moral rights and invests the responsibility of punishment in the State and its laws, which embody the collective strength
of the community. Clearly, the purpose of the Lockean State and its laws is to protect
the citizen's natural or moral rights that are pre-existent to the State. Hence, the State
does not create fundamental moral rights; nor does it create fundamental moral obligations; rather it enforces such rights against those who are inclined to violate them.[6]
Important to individuals' liberty and pursuit of happiness are "institutional affilia-

tions" or choices that individuals of maturity make to relate to others in the context of relationships defined by social structures that have developed over time quite independently of the State. Included here are such institutions or structures as the family, the church/synagogue/temple, the trades and professions, service and "civic" organizations, and so on. From this perspective, institutional affiliations develop and express moral character independently by and large of the State.

The separation of (religious) morality and state is not only of fundamental conceptual importance, it is crucial to the integrity of each and to one's being an ethical or conscientious citizen. If we presume that it is the liberal, democratic state that defines communal values, then whatever the law permits would be morally acceptable; and so, if it is not the "law's business" whether we regard our fellows with good will and propriety, then we are "free" not to so care for others. On the other hand, if it is compassion that defines our communal values, then it should become the "business" of public policy to assure that people's basic human needs and dignity are addressed. So, while citizens should enjoy a broad sphere of privacy, i.e., rights not to be interfered with or "harmed" by others, in order to live their lives according to their talents and interests, public resources also should ensure that its citizens are not deprived, so far as "practically possible," of normal human capacities and opportunities. On this view, "unfettered individualism," or "libertarianism" should be eschewed in so far as it fosters and protects our collective "right" not to care about others. (Garfield, 1995:15)

The separation of moral conscience from state authority also renders all political distinctions, distinctions based on political power and interests, irrelevant to the determination of one's responsibilities based upon authentic moral precepts and practices. If the moral law is "Thou shalt not kill" or "Abstain from the taking of life," it is irrelevant, it seems to me, whether we are talking about the life of a "fellow countryman" or the life of any other human being. It follows also that the moral precepts that apply in one's role as a "public" authority are identical to those that apply in one's life as a "private" citizen.

There is a popular saying, "There cannot be peace without justice." As we have seen, to refrain from harming others and to benefit others in need is justice. In this sense, being at peace presumes just relationships. In order for a state of peace to be established directly between two parties, each party minimally must be a justice-bearer in the sense of not wishing harm on anyone and being prepared to do good for those disposed to do good. Some people say that justice first must be achieved in order, subsequently, for peace to be established, and what sometimes they have in mind by "justice" is "compensatory" or "rectifactory" justice ("retribution"), that one side must pay off a debt of injustice to the other side; but usually, the side against whom such a claim is made counters that its actions were in legitimate response to yet prior injustices on the part of the other side; and so on. To *demand* "compensatory" or "retribution" is evidence of a state of war; it is not a path to peace. On this view, to even expect recompense in the future as a condition of "peace" is to remain in a state of hostility or ill will. Establishing a state of peace, says Kant, "nullifies all existing causes of war, even if they are unknown to the contracting parties". (Kant, 1983:109)

However, establishing peace is exceedingly difficult when one party does not demonstrate a readiness to give up what it sees as a "just cause" for hostility, since it has been deeply wounded and cannot let go of its suffering. Simone Weil offers this prescription for those who might maintain justice:

> For those to whom harm has been done, it means to efface the material consequences by putting them in a place where the wound, if it is not too deep, may be cured naturally by a spell of well-being. But for those in whom the wound is a laceration of the soul it means further, and above all, to offer them good in its purest form to assuage their thirst. (Weil, 1977:335)

Perhaps individuals—with like minded friends and fellow citizens—taking a public vow to be nonviolent and to work for the benefit of all would constitute a way to begin to establish a culture of peace in our communities and beyond.

Right Subsistence

An ethic of compassion provides a three-fold basis for environmental consciousness. First, the commitment not to cause sentient beings to suffer, along with both an understanding of how the weal and woe of sentient beings are dependent upon complex environmental conditions and an awareness of how our individual and collective behaviors affect the environment, commits one to protect, preserve and/or restore environmental conditions conducive to the support of life. Second, the notion of "deep ecology" captures the compassionate heart's impartiality in fostering the integrity of all beings:

> deep ecology is a mentality in which all beings are seen as having equal rights to their own forms of unfolding and realization within their biosphere....Deep ecology is about the cultivation of a consciousness so that, in Arne Naess's words, 'with maturity, human beings will experience joy when other life forms experience joy, and sorrow when other life forms experience sorrow'. . . . Deep ecology requires us to be aware and responsible and yet at the same time a force of nature, a selfless phenomenon of the ecological process—we who *have to think* about what we should do. (Jones, 1989:139)

And, third, this form of awareness reflects one's openness to being, to *simply* acknowledging and letting things be what they are; this is a profound practice of generosity and patience.

In Chapter I, compassion was introduced through the Golden Rule; and, while most people assume that the Golden Rule only extends to other human beings or to other moral agents, this restriction is arbitrary. In Desmond Stewart's "The Limits of Trooghaft" (1972), the reader is confronted with a race of extraordinarily intelligent, powerful and gigantic beings who come to master planet earth and then divide its human inhabitants ("*homo insipiens*") into four castes: "housemen" (pets), capons (raised for food), hound-men (bred for speed, obedience and ruthlessness) and quarrymen (wild game, but subject to various kinds of study and experimentation). The obvious lesson lies in terms of something like the Golden Rule; the reader certainly objects to human beings being treated in the ways depicted, and, so, since one would not wish to be so treated, (perhaps) one should not be treating animals in the ways that are commonly accepted by current norms.

Then, too, "environmental benevolence" can extend beyond higher animals and include plant life, habitats and eco-systems. That this occurs, for the Buddhist, is a natural result of seeing oneself, not as having a self-same, independent "identity," but as having "dependent origination," as arising out of a myriad of causes and conditions, as "inter-being." In observing how we are dependent upon our environment, and how our environment is dependent upon us, we learn that to take care of the one is tied up with taking care of the other; and, so we learn how to take care of both in their mutuality.

> What can make the extension of concern to nonhuman others more likely is the realization that the flourishing of one's self and that of others occurs in, and is made possible by, an extended environmental community. This, in turn, requires the recognition that the notion of community must be expanded to include nonhuman entities, both living and non-living. (Frasz, 2005:126)

While Buddhist writers even talk of "the world as self" and "the greening of the self" (e.g., Macy, 1991), from a more traditional Western perspective it is readily apparent that one's responsibilities extend through our environment by reflecting on what we consider to be vices—e.g., greed, carelessness, disrespect, apathy, and arrogance—and how they can characterize human attitudes and conduct with respect to the nonhuman world. One can as well greedily "take what is not given" from nature, thus destroying an entire habitat, as well as from a family, thus impoverishing them. Put otherwise, the kind of mindfulness appropriate to fulfilling one's responsibilities of aspiration naturally extends to whatever environment one finds oneself in.

The human task is to live in the mindfulness of the universal dimensions of our individual and collective conduct. Such awareness is more readily sustained in a life led simply. Right livelihood and right subsistence should be practiced in a manner that both provides for the necessities of life and allows one to focus on living according to the precepts of moral aspiration as well as the precepts of moral duty. Each moral agent is responsible for being a protector of earth and humanity.

> Thus, for every single thing that lives,
> In number like the boundless reaches of the sky,
> May I be their sustenance and nourishment
> Until they pass beyond bounds of suffering.
>
> Shantideva, 1997, 3.22

3. Selflessness and Desirelessness

Sometimes it is thought that the fully compassionate person must be totally selfless and that this requires that one be completely desireless since all desires are rooted in an egoistic self-centeredness incompatible with being fully compassionate. The aim of this section is to indicate that being compassionate manifests in intentional conduct; and, since intentional conduct may be analyzable in terms of "belief + desire," there is no necessity for a fully compassionate person to be void of all desire. Furthermore, the fully compassionate person wishes for the alleviation of the suffering of *all* beings; and since "all beings" includes oneself, one may act with self-regarding as well as other-regarding intentions. In the following appendix, I argue that the so-called "paradox of desire" does not have roots in the Buddha's teachings on how one may become liberated from suffering.

Bart Gruzalski (2000:Ch.7) recently has proposed a distinction that he thinks can explain "action without desire." It may seem that habitual actions are actions without felt, occurrent desires; for example, the ways in which we start and drive a car, do our morning bath, answer the phone, and so on, might be so routinely done that we do not experience any desire in doing them the way we do. Yet, as Gruzalski points out, such behaviors are rooted in desire, both in how we came to adopt the routines we have and with respect to the goals that such routines accomplish. In so far as our routines are merely habitual, Gruzalski points out, they certainly can lead to frustration as when they are not effective in achieving our goals. For instance, a person who gardens in habitual ways may be frustrated when unusual weather patterns prevent her from achieving the desired results. However, a person who gardens skillfully will follow certain principles but will be quite flexible in their application; moreover, an enlightened, skillful gardener would not be attached to goals and would be able to accept what arises.

> As long as she is only trying to garden skillfully and is not attached to the results, she will no more be frustrated when she needs to cover her tomato plants at night for another week than she would be if, while only trying to play skillfully, she lost her most skillful game of chess to a player whom she knew to be much better than herself. (Gruzalski, 2000:66)

Gruzalski claims that "acting skillfully" may account for "coherent patterns of human activity unmotivated by desire" even though they typically occur in contexts in which desire plays a fundamental motivational role. Persons who garden skillfully are typically motivated by a desire for a supply of fresh produce, to consume or to sell; most skillful chess players are motivated by a desire to win or to do well in competition. We are quite familiar with this teaching that bids us to remain in the present: when eating, eat, that is, just eat; when cooking, cook; when fishing, fish. If one engages in the activity fully, not attached to results, then we might say that there is no underlying, goal-directed desire that might be the basis for one's satisfaction or dissatisfaction. Even so, such activity is not totally "desireless" since it is intentional. What accounts for the underlying *pattern* of a skillful activity is the agent's intentionality; and, as Gruzalski himself recognizes, philosophers often analyze intention in terms of belief + desire.[7] The person who is "just fishing" intends to fish, and this accounts for the activities of tying flies, wading, casting, and so on, even if she is not intent on or attached to the goal of catching and eating a fish. Of course, the activity of fishing may result in catching a fish; but, without the goal of catching a fish, one will not be disappointed in not doing so and one will be more open to ceasing to fish if another activity would be more appropriate for the circumstances.[8]

Even if it were possible to engage in skillful activities without desire, Gruzalski wonders (66), "Is it possible for an entire life to be devoid of desire?" As much as one might wish, I should think, fishing (golfing, gardening, running Microsoft, or whatever) cannot constitute or embrace one's entire life; the question may always arise, "Why fish (eat, sit, garden, etc.) *now*?" In any event, Gruzalski proposes that it is in the possibility of one's being fully compassionate that we can find a life devoid of desire.

> Once one is fully compassionate, there is never an occasion for frustration over the suffering of others. If one can do something to relieve the suffering of another, and this is the overall compassionate act, one does so. If there is suffering that cannot be relieved, that cannot be relieved, an understanding of this reality would prevent frustration or any other suffering for a fully compassionate person....In all of this, because being compassionate requires alertness and allaying suffering with ones [sic] own being, the compassionate person will care for her mind, heart, and body. Likewise, because being compassionate requires being in relation to others, the compassionate person will nourish noble friendships, and her ties to her family and the various communities of which she is a member. In these ways compassion may inform and guide an entire life. (Gruzalski, 2000:67)

That compassion may guide and embrace an entire life, all of one's energies, and that one who is fully compassionate is not motivated by or attached to the attainment of results, does not entail that one's life is desireless, since all intentional actions are motivated at least in the sense that the agent wants to do them for their own sake if not for the sake of some result to be thereby attained.

Of course, a difficulty arises when one considers the possibility of the egocentric adept who engages in spiritual practices to transform himself into a fully compassionate being. Must not these efforts be motivated by the desire to attain the goal of becoming fully compassionate? (And, further, for the Buddhist, might not this be one's goal since one wishes for oneself to pass beyond suffering, i.e., to attain liberation?) How is it that one can become non-attached to results or goals if one is, all the while, being motivated to attain a result or goal for oneself?

The path of the bodhisattva in training provides a way out of this paradox. Part of the bodhisattva vow proclaims: "For the ultimate benefit of all beings, without exception, throughout this and all my lifetimes, I dedicate myself to the practice and realization of enlightenment until all together reach that goal." The "goal" here is not "self-liberation" but the "liberation of all beings." Often the Bodhisattvayāna is expressed by the phrase, "one seeks enlightenment for the sake of all sentient beings;" this aspiration is "relative *bodhichitta*" or "awakened mind." It is common to distinguish two forms of "relative *bodhicitta*"—aspiration (intention) and application, e.g., through such practices as the "exchange of self and other" and the six transcendental virtues (*paramitas*). (Shantideva, 1997) Perfection of application culminates in wisdom, or the "realization of (reality as) emptiness" which is "absolute *bodhichitta*." The bodhisattva practices, in short, bring one to the realization of the emptiness (or inter-dependencies) of self and others, so that one may be equally responsive to the sufferings of all and be as intent to alleviate others' sufferings as one would one's own. One becomes self-less, ego-less, not by pursuing a goal for oneself but by pursuing the liberation from suffering of all beings. Moreover, the person who becomes *fully* compassionate, as Gruzalski points out, does not act deliberatively to conform to an ideal; rather compassion "is just one's nature, the way one is." (Gruzalski, 2000:67)

Just helping beings in need is what compassionate beings do, "without thinking," "naturally," and without discrimination or agenda. There is not even an "attachment" to the "fate" of the victim, e.g., whether he recovers from his injuries or not, even though one does all that what one can do under the circumstances. Yet, being *fully* compassionate does not seem so straight-forward, so "natural" for us. "Just helping" a being in need is something we all do "naturally" *on occasion*. Yet, we do not find ourselves living a life that "*just* helps beings in need," that is, is always open and responsive to the needs of beings (others and ourselves). Whereas we might "just sit" on occasion, it is not so easy to "just sit" as an ongoing practice. Similarly, for some, "just breathing is the meditation;" but, how often does one "just breathe?" While sitting or breathing is natural and easy, *just* sitting or *just* breathing is not easy for us; similarly, *just* helping others seems perplexingly difficult. Why? Because we are not capable or ready to "let go" of all other agenda, of our having a "goal-seeking desiring mind." And, living in our "everyday" world, amidst its mundane concerns, makes such "letting go" a practical impossibility for most of us. Thus, Shakyamuni Buddha observes, "While living at home, it is not so easy to live the higher spiritual life that is completely fulfilled and completely pure like a polished shell," and he proceeds to delineate the ways in which the *bhikkhu*'s renunciations and trainings lead to the cessation of craving and, thus, of suffering. (Buddha, 2006:69ff) So, achieving moral perfection, becoming fully compassionate, remains for most persons an "ideal;" still, it is attainable, but only with renunciation. Nevertheless, the ideal offers a standard against which to measure one's conduct and oneself.

In sum, a fully compassionate person simply lives; her openness or responsiveness manifests compassion spontaneously in her conduct; nevertheless, since even spontaneously generated conduct is intentional, we cannot say that a liberated person-in-the-world is entirely desireless. However, we can say that such a person's desires are neither self-directed nor goal directed beyond the aspiration to free all beings from suffering.[9] That a compassionate person is "selfless" means, in the Buddhist tradition, that she manifests the nature of being human. Selflessness is our nature; but most of us act under the illusion of an ego-identity that we cherish and, so, seek to preserve and enhance. Chapter VI.3-4 seeks to explain the grounds for holding "selfless" agents morally accountable.

4. Appendix: For the Buddhist, Does the Cessation of Suffering Require Desirelessness?

In an insightful pair of essays, John Visader (1978) and A.L. Herman (1979) develop three claims.[10]

> 1. Buddhism has as one of its chief aims the "cessation" of desires and desiring, which is to say the "extinction" of desires or, in other words, the attainment of the "state of desirelessness."
> 2. However, there is a very real paradox ("the paradox of desire") here, since one who aims at liberation from suffering can become desireless only if he should so desire; but, in so far as one desires to eliminate all desires, desire can never be eliminated.
> 3. Hence, becoming desireless is achievable only through practices that do not have as their direct intention the elimination of all desires.

It seems that the issue of the possibility of one's becoming desireless is of general concern for Western commentators on Buddhism. The problem arises this way. According to Buddha's teachings on the Four Noble Truths, since suffering arises due to *tanha*, often translated as "desire," then the cessation of suffering requires the cessation or elimination of *tanha*. This sets up the claim that there is a "paradox of desire" in Buddhism.

In his original article, John Visader claims that Buddhism has as one of its chief aims the "extinction of desire" without qualification (Visader, 1978:461) and A.L. Herman specifically rejects any attempt to distinguish between desires that should be eliminated from those which need not be, because, he says, "Buddhists themselves seem to reject it." (Herman, 1979:92) In a subsequent article, however, Visader makes a crucial parting observation:

> The word "desire" as used by Buddhists is a technical philosophical term and is not coextensive with the ordinary use of that word in English. It is to be expected that an enlightened person, being free of such things as *graha, kama, klesa* and *trsna*, will still desire to do such things as drink tea, go for a walk, or help other people. (Visader, 1980:534)

"*Grāha*" is the Sanskrit equivalent of the Pali term, "*tanha*." And, indeed, is not Shakyamuni Buddha the exemplar of a liberated being who acted intentionally, compassionately, and hence with desire in at least some sense?

In the *Discourse on Right View*, Buddha Shakyamuni is recorded as saying:

> ".... Birth is suffering; aging is suffering; sickness is suffering; death is suffering; sorrow, lamentation, pain, grief and despair are suffering; not to obtain what one wants is suffering; in short, the five aggregates affected by clinging are suffering. This is called suffering.

"And what is the origin of suffering? It is craving, which brings renewal of being, is accompanied by delight and lust, and delights in this and that; that is, craving for sensual pleasures, craving for being and craving for non-being. This is called the origin of suffering.
"And what is the cessation of suffering? It is the remainderless fading away and ceasing, the giving up, relinquishing, letting go and rejecting of that same craving. This is called the cessation of suffering." (Buddha, 1991:15-17)

It seems clear that the cause of suffering is said to be "clinging" or "craving" (as *grāha* and *tanha* may be rendered) and not "desire" more generally.[11] The essential teaching here seems (at least to me) to be that the cessation of suffering lies in one's being free *from* desire rather than in being free *of* desire. A person who is utterly desireless would have no basis for intending "the giving up, relinquishing, letting go and rejecting of that same craving." In realizing the "emptiness" of the object of desire, there is nothing to dwell on; in realizing the emptiness of one's desire, it is therein let go of and one is liberated from it. In the realization of the emptiness of all things, there is no grasping or thirsting for "objects of desire" and, so, there is no "desiring mind" in this sense.

In the discourse *Feelings That Should Be Seen and the Dart* (*Samyutta Nikāya* 4.207-210), The Buddha clearly teaches that the difference between an ordinary person and a noble disciple who both experience a pleasant feeling, a painful feeling, or a neither-painful-nor-pleasant feeling, is that the latter "feels it as a person who is detached from it." The Buddha's main teaching here is that the unlearned ordinary person when touched by an unpleasant feeling or by a pleasant feeling, experiences a corresponding second, mental feeling, i.e., one of either aversion or craving, which are sources of suffering. On the other hand,

One who has fathomed the *dhamma*,
A person of great learning,
Sees the world with this difference:
Such a person's mind is not disturbed by pleasing things
Nor by undesirable things is that person repulsed.

By one's disinclination, dislike, and opposition
They are scattered, extinguished, and exist no more.
Having understood the reason
One is free from stain and sorrow
One understands rightly and has gone beyond becoming. (Buddha, 2006:93-94)

Further, in this context, to experience a pleasant feeling includes the experience of an object as pleasant, to experience a pleasing feeling towards it; and this is not far from experiencing an object as desirable, to experience a desire for it. In *The Greater Discourse on the Destruction of Craving* (*Mahātanhāsankhaya*, 13-15) The Buddha describes a youth as enjoying himself with sense-feelings and mental objects "that are wished for, desirable, pleasing, enticing, connected with pleasure, and exciting." (Buddha, 2006:68) In Western philosophy, it is common to define what is judged "good" as what is "desirable." But, in The Buddha's teachings, pleasant feelings, and even objects of pleasant feelings, are not "good" simply in so far as such feelings are pleasant or in so far as pleasing objects are desirable. John J. Holder summarizes The Buddha's teaching this way:

> According to the Buddha's detailed causal analysis of the arising and cessation of suffering, craving arises at the most critical juncture. In the ordinary, corrupted mind, craving arises as a result of feeling (*vedanā*). By themselves, feelings are neither good nor bad—they are merely pleasant, painful, or neutral. But when feelings are filtered through a defiled mind, a person reacts to feelings by developing cravings that invariably lead to suffering. In contrast, a person having a liberated or morally purified mind reacts to feelings by developing wholesome mental states like equanimity and dispassion that lead to tranquility and happiness. (Buddha, 2006:59)

We might say, for example, that a "lustful" person is one who takes delight in pleasant feelings, who favors the pursuit of pleasure, who, in short, judges pleasure as "good;" similarly, a "worrisome" person is one who has an aversion to painful feelings, whose interest is captured by the expectation of painful feelings, who favors the avoidance of painful feelings, who, in short, judges pain as "bad." One way of understanding this is to take the experience of a pleasing feeling towards an object as akin to a "first-order desire" to wish for or to have that object; and, to take the experience of a painful feeling about something as akin to a "first-order desire" to be free from that thing. "Second-order desires" have as their object first-order desires; they are desires (or preferences) to have or not to have particular "first-order desires" constitute our ego-will, be the bases of our conduct.[12] Ordinary-minded people reinforce their "first-order desires" by "second-order desires" whereby they favor some and oppose others on the basis of their "judgments" of what is "good" or "bad." Such second-order desires are the "mental dispositions" ("dispositional desires") rooted in one's ignorance of the true nature of self and phenomena. Extraordinary-minded people are free from such second-order dispositions. If one is trained to "let go" of first-order desires, to favor neither the pursuit of what is pleasing nor the avoidance of what is painful, then these desires are "extinguished." In The Buddha's words:

> And so having abandoned favoring and opposing whatever feeling he feels—whether it is pleasant or painful or neither-painful-nor pleasant—he does not delight in that feeling, he does not welcome it, and he does not remain attached to it. As he does not do so, delight in feeling ceases in him. From the cessation of delight in feeling, attachment ceases...Thus ceases this whole mass of suffering. (Buddha, 2006:72)

Just as in meditation, one may have passing thoughts without "thinking" on or "holding" to them, so too "objects of desire" may pass by without being "held" or "craved." That is to say, to be "non-thinking" does not entail that one is void of thought or "thoughtless;" and, similarly, to say that one is non-desiring does not entail that one is void of desire or "desireless." With insight-awareness, in being aware they are nearly instantaneously self-liberated.

In sum, I do not believe that there is a "paradox of desire" in Buddhism since I do not think that Buddhism teaches that if one aspires to liberation from suffering then one *must* desire to attain the goal of desirelessness. A person who no longer is subject to suffering (to karma) need not be utterly desireless since such a person characteristically engages (only) in intentional conduct to benefit sentient beings. Further, even if being free from suffering means that one is free from the results of action, and hence from goal-directed desires, this does not mean that one both must have had and fulfilled a desire specifically to be free of goal-directed desires. There are many paths to enlightenment. The possibilities include one's encountering the utter practical impossibility of attaining happiness through the fulfillment of desires and, hence, one's just "giving up" one's desiring mind, as Professor Herman described.[13] And, they also include the Bodhisattvayāna in which one gives rise to, maintains and perfects the aspiration to free all beings from suffering. Moreover, it seems to me, one's being free of a desiring mind means that one is free of dispositional, second-orders and that this enables one to be free from, to extinguish, whatever "feelings" or first-order desires one may have. In any case, since being compassionate is the manifestation of the realization of the true nature of reality, and since being compassionate means that one intentionally acts for the benefit of beings, and since one cannot act intentionally without desire or aspiration, we may conclude: "No, desirelessness is not desirable."

NOTES

1. The following two paragraphs are adopted from Richard Reilly, 1977b:101-2; all page references in these paragraphs refer to the *Gorgias*. For an explication of the conceptual relations that underpin Socrates' reasoning, see Santas, 1964.

2. The Dalai Lama (1999, Ch. 4-5) conceives of happiness as "inner peace" and provides an eloquent explanation of how a life of happiness results from a life of virtue.

3. For an interesting discussion of this see Wilkes (1980); Rorty (1980) argues that Aristotle's two views of the end of the good life are compatible.

4. These summaries borrow extensively from commentaries by Trungpa (1993) and Hanh (1998, Ch. 25).

5. The roots of this subordination of conscience are uncovered in the *Crito* where Socrates imagines the laws making a case for his obedience and thus for his accepting the death penalty.

> What complaint have you against us and the state, that you are trying to destroy us? Are we not, first of all, your parents? Through us your father took your mother and brought you into the world. Tell us, have you any fault to find with those of us who are the laws of marriage? "I have none,' I should reply. 'Or have any fault with those of us that regulate the raising of the child and the education which you, like others, received? . . . Well, then, since you were brought into the world and raised and educated by us, how, in the first place, can you deny that you are our child and our slave, as your fathers were before you? And if this be so, do you think that your rights are on a level with ours?' (Plato, 1956:60)

On this view, the institutions which develop and express moral character and personal identity are defined and protected by the laws of the State. Moreover, if the State and its laws are thought to be divinely instituted, as the Old Testament proclaims and as *Romans* 13 suggests, the subordination of individual moral conscience to moral authority is greatly reinforced.

Fortunately, in neither theory nor circumstance does this classical model of the State pertain to our time. John Stuart Mill remarked in *On Liberty*:

> The ancient commonwealths thought themselves entitled to practice, and the ancient philosophers countenanced the regulation of every part of private conduct by public authority, on the ground that the State had a deep interest in the whole bodily and mental discipline of every one of its citizens. . . . In the modern world, the greater size of political communities, and, above all, the separation between spiritual and temporal authority (which placed the direction of men's conscience in other hands than those which controlled their worldly affairs), prevented so great an interference by law in the details of private life. (Mill, 1947:13)

6. For this general view, see John Locke, *The Second Treatise on Government*. In Ch. II.6 Locke states: "The state of Nature has a law of Nature to govern it, which obliges everyone, and reason, which is that law, teaches all mankind who but will consult it, that being all equal and independent, no one ought to harm another in his life, health, liberty or possessions...." (Locke, 1952:5) On Locke's view, the parties to the social contract are the individuals themselves—they agree with one another to establish political authority responsible to their collective will; it is not the case here that individuals *qua* citizens are parties to a contract with the State that their agreement brings into existence.

7. The strong (and problematic) claim is that intentions are reducible to complexes of beliefs and desires; this view is argued forcefully by Audi (1973). In any case, as a leading non-reductivist states, "There is, predictably, considerable agreement that intentions are closely linked to desires and beliefs. It is generally recognized that intentions have a motivational dimension and 'desire' (like 'want') is often used in the literature as an umbrella term for motivation." (Mele, 1997:17) That actions are guided by intentions (or plans) does seem to presume that an agent's (conscious) intentional actions manifest a preference or (dispositional) desire of the agent; for an account of such preferences, see Reilly (1979b).

8. On May 25, 2006, *The Washington Post* reported that a fallen climber, David Sharp, lacking oxygen, died on May 15th after some forty other climbers passed by him on their way to ascend Mt. Everest. While these climbers were deeply dwelling in their activity of climbing, clearly they were attached to the achievement of a goal. In *Miracle of Mindfulness*, Thich Nhat Hanh advises that when washing the dishes, just wash the dishes without even the goal of cleaning them! Between drafts of this section, I spent some time weeding the stone sidewalk leading to my house. In doing so, I disturbed numerous sentient beings, including ants, mother spiders with their eggs, and various types of worms, a couple of which were (accidentally) disabled. So, how is one to "just help beings" if one is acting with *other* goals or purposes?

9. It should be kept in mind that the aspiration of liberating numberless sentient beings "throughout all my lifetimes" cannot be envisioned as a determinate "goal." What this means and requires of us is "indeterminate" *par excellance*; it is not a standard by which one might measure one's "progress," let alone anticipate completing, in "the here and now" of action.

10. A critique of these articles was published in *Philosophy East and West* 30.4 with rejoinders by Herman (1980) and Visader (1980).

11. Huston Smith (1991, 102) rejects the translation of *tanha* as "desire," for reasons similar to those mentioned in this volume. Smith's influential view is that the goal of the Buddhist devotee is to overcome self-interestedness, to no longer have "the desire for private ful-

fillment." This is so, but the problem goes a bit deeper than Smith's analysis suggests. First, the intention to give up all self-interested desires may yet be rooted in a "self" that is seeking some goal, e.g. "liberation;" must not even this desire be given up for one to become truly "liberated?" Second, it appears that the root of suffering lies in the pursuit of goals generally, whether they deal with "private fulfillment" or are "altruistic." What I argue is that the self-lessness that characterizes the fully compassionate person requires that one is not attached to "goals" but that this does not require desirelessness. See note 7 supra. Similarly, in the Christian tradition, Augustine claims that the root of sin is "lust" by which he means "inordinate (unlawful) desire" and not "desire" *simpliciter*. See Saint Augustine, 1993, *On Free Choice of the Will*, I. 3-4, 11-13. The Western philosophical notion of "desire" captures broadly any "motivation" one may have for doing what one does. "Paradoxes of desire," as well as religious condemnations of "desire," often are rooted in equivocations on the term.

12. I here follow the influential view of Harry Frankfurt (1971); this view is elaborated upon in Chapter VI.2-3.

13. Visader instructively distinguishes three stages in the "dialectic of emptiness."

> the first is the emptiness of the self and the potential objects of clinging....In the second stage the emptiness of the doctrine is asserted, while the third stage points out the emptiness of emptiness itself....Once the emptiness of the doctrine and practice are asserted, then the craving mind does not have anything to cling to and thus its latest stronghold is exposed. This is where one is confronted with the desire to give up desires. (Visader, 1978:463)

What I understand Visader to mean when he concludes, "This is where one is confronted with the desire to give up desires" is decidedly not, "This is where one is confronted with the desire to give up the actual, particular desires one has" but rather "This is where one is confronted with the desire to give up the desiring mind one has." But, of course, is not the desire to give up desiring self-defeating? Herman captures nicely the predicament of the devotee:

> seeing that there is no way out of the paradox of desire, understanding that as Mād-haymika [sic] Buddhism puts it, there is no way to *nirvāna*, no goal to be desired or achieved, then one "lets go" of the way and the goal. And that "letting go" leads to or is *nirvāna*: For once the devotee realizes that there is nothing he can do then there is nothing left to be done. (Herman, 1979:93-94)

In other words, only when one both faces up to the point that all desiring is self-defeating, utterly useless, might one just "give up" desiring altogether. But here, becoming desireless is not achieved by directly acting on a desire to become or to remain desireless. And, of course, it is not necessary for one to travel this path to reach *nirvāna*.

Chapter VI
Will, Responsibility and Selflessness

We are left alone, without excuse. That is what I mean when I say that man is condemned to be free. Condemned, because he did not create himself, yet is nevertheless at liberty, and from the moment that he is thrown into this world he is responsible for everything he does.

Jean-Paul Sartre, "Existentialism is a Humanism"

We have seen that being compassionate requires one to be (more or less) "selfless." It is well known that Buddhism rejects the notion that human beings (as well as "objects") possess an inherent, independent "identity," that is, are what I term "concrete individuals." That persons (and objects) lack such a nature is what is meant when Mahāyāna Buddhists say that they are "empty," i.e., void of "permanently, self-same" existence." So, on the Mahāyāna view, living in the recognition of one's nature as self-less or "empty" is manifested in one's being compassionate. This raises an interesting and important issue: how are "free will" and "personal responsibility" compatible with the view that moral agents do not have "concrete identities?" And, further, how is all this compatible with the notion that the situations that one finds oneself in may be a result of "karma?" By addressing these issues, we will put to rest the suspicion that the view that agents are "selfless" is incompatible with "moral agency" and, so, with an ethic of compassion.[1]

The philosophical issues surrounding "free will" have received an enormous amount of attention from Western philosophers over the past half-century; it is not my aim here to sift through the thicket of complex arguments and counter-arguments that have been produced.[2] Rather, what I wish to point out is how the standard "compatibilist" view of free action presumes that human beings possess a rather stable "character" ("individuality" or "self"); moreover, compatibilists also hold the related view that were it not for the fact that one's free actions proceed from one's self, we could not explain coherently the notion of holding one responsible (accountable, blameworthy or praiseworthy) for doing what one does. I will illustrate these themes by reference to Aristotle, who was the first to articulate a compatibilist conception of free action for which one is responsible. I then will show why these compatibilist intuitions are questionable. In Section 2 we will review first the pivotal movement away from an Aristotelian view of agency to a "libertarian" view brought about by St. Augustine and then take note of Jean-Paul Sartre's claim that the existence of human freedom means that human agents are "selfless." That freedom and responsibility are compatible with agent-selflessness also means that they are compatible with the notion that the "life-situation" one acts within is a "given" or one's "karma." The task in Section 3 is to develop a libertarian account of free-will that (a) does not presume that an agent's free choices emanate from a formed character or from settled dispositions, but, nevertheless, (b) does offer a responsibility-conferring concept of agent-control that is consistent with the intuition that free agents have the capacity to rationally act (choose) otherwise than they do. Section 4 then explains how agents who make their choices ("judgments of preference") "freely" and "rationally" are "responsible" for their choices and for actions that result willfully from them. This chapter concludes with an overview in Section 5 of how "praise" and "blame," as well as "reward" and "punishment," should be construed within the framework of an ethics of compassion.

1. Aristotle on Practical Agency

Aristotle was the first to distinguish systematically those acts for which one is responsible (i.e., a fit subject of praise and blame) from those acts for which one is not responsible. His general view (*Nic. Eth.* III, 1-5) is that a person is not responsible for those acts which he commits owing to ignorance, i.e., in ignorance of the particular features of the circumstance of action which are crucial to defining the nature of the act, or which take place under compulsion. Ignorance and involuntariness rule out choice, for one cannot be said to choose or willfully intend to do what he does not know that he is doing or what he is compelled to do regardless of his own preferences or wants. Furthermore, on Aristotelian doctrine, the ignorance or compulsion that exculpates must be such that the agent suffers it in a non-culpable manner. The Anglo-American legal tradition pays homage to Aristotle's account of moral responsibility by the maxim: *Actus non tacit reum, nise mens sit rea* – "The act alone does not amount to guilt, it must be accompanied by a guilty mind." Excepting special cases involving either "strict liability" statutes or "inadvertent negligence," the law does not punish persons who commit prohibited acts either done in ignorance (e.g., as with accidents) or done involuntarily (*i.e.*, where the agent does not exercise rational control).

In short, it is "choice" that renders the Aristotelian agent "responsible." Acts are "voluntary" if the moving principle (e.g., a desire or motive) is within the agent. "Since that which is done under compulsion or by reason of ignorance is involuntary, the voluntary would seem to be that of which the moving principle is in the agent himself, he being aware of the particular circumstance of the action." (*Nic. Eth.*, 1111a20-25) While involuntariness rules out culpability, voluntariness does not guarantee it. As Aristotle noted, "the vices that are blamed must be in our power" (*Nic. Eth.*, 1114a25-35) and while animals and toddlers act voluntarily (e.g., in acting appetitively), their actions are not proper objects of praise and blame. Involuntariness rules out "choice," which characterizes a subset of voluntary actions.

> Choice, then, seems to be voluntary but not the same as the voluntary; the latter extends more widely. For both children and the lower animals share in voluntary action, but not in choice, and acts done on the spur of the moment we describe as voluntary, but not as chosen. . . . Choice is not common to irrational creatures as well, but appetite and anger are. (*Nic. Eth.*, 1111b5-15)

The reason why choice is not common to irrational creatures, for Aristotle, is that he holds that choice is embedded in one's judgments of what he or she should be doing, and these judgments reflect the application of general principles to the circumstances in which one finds oneself. On Aristotle's view, practical reasoning (the "practical syllogism") has two primary components—a "major premise" that describes a type of action that is or is not desirable (conducive to happiness) and a minor premise that reflects one's recognition (perceptual belief) that now is an occasion for performing or not that kind of act; the combination of these premises leads to one's acting "straight away" (if one is not constrained) which is the same as judging, "I shall do this!" The consideration, adoption and application of general principles, such as "It is good [desirable] to be kind" or "It is good to pursue sensual pleasures," requires a degree of rational thinking that the lower animals do not evidence.

We saw in Chapter V that Aristotelian virtues and vices are states of character and states of character are habits or dispositions which normally result from processes of habituation in one's youth. The virtuous person adopts and lives by "good" principles that lead to conduct that reflects an excellence of character because that conduct is conducive to a fulfilling (successful, happy) life; whereas vices are tied to "wrong principles" in that the behavior they endorse leads one away from a fulfilling (successful, happy) life. Aristotle's general view, then, is that one is to be held responsible (blameworthy or praiseworthy) for those acts that stem from a disposition or general principle within one's power not to have; and, while it may not always be in one's power not to have (or not to act upon) a settled disposition that marks one's identity, it was in his or her power not to have engaged in those behaviors which account for the development, and hence for the current existence, of one's dispositions.

Compatibilists seek to explain free acts in a manner consistent with acts being causally determined. Aristotle's account offers such a vehicle. Free acts stem from the confluence of one's dispositions/principles, which establish what kinds of conduct are desirable and undesirable for an agent, together with one's beliefs about the circumstances in which one finds oneself and how these circumstances provide opportunities to exercise one's principles.[3] Different individuals who have similar beliefs about the circumstances they face (choose to) act differently because of their differences of character, that is, differences in dispositional tendencies which, in turn, reflect differences in how they have internalized general principles about what is desirable (good) and undesirable (bad). That a person who did a wicked (vicious) act yesterday should be he held to account (blamed, punished) tomorrow can only be explained, argue compatibilists, on the assumption that the bad disposition (vice) that manifested in the agent's conduct of yesterday remains in the agent tomorrow, otherwise what is it about the agent tomorrow that deserves blame or punishment and what is it that the blame or punishment is to accomplish if not to condemn and even alter or counteract the (same) disposition evidenced in the wrongful conduct?

There is, however, a two-fold difficulty with a dispositional analysis of agent-responsibility. On the one hand, it remains unclear how one is responsible for the harmful dispositions that one has developed and which now are constitutive of one's identity. Since, for Aristotle, rational agents choose what they do believing that it is conducive to their own "good," it must be that ignorance of what kinds of things are so conducive accompanies one's "wrongful choices" and "harmful behaviors" that, over time, lead to harmful habituations and dispositions. It may be that poor role models, lax social standards, ineffective education, and so on, account for the "ignorance" of youths' bad choices; but, in any case, it is difficult on Aristotle's account to explain how such ignorance is something for which the agents themselves are responsible. (Nor does Aristotle's account lend itself readily to the possibility of one's freely undoing the wrongful dispositions.) And, on the other hand, Aristotle's account does not allow for us to hold agents responsible for conduct that is "out of character," for example, as Aristotle notes, done "on the spur of the moment," for while such conduct might be voluntary it is not "chosen" since it does not accord with one's adopted principles and formed dispositions. This is an acute problem for Aristotle, who recognized that the weak-willed individual who acts against his better judgment is blameworthy but, yet, does not act "from choice." So, how is his "blameworthiness" to be explained?[4]

2. "Free Choice of the Will," "Selflessness," and "Karma"

St. Augustine came to write systematically on "free choice of the will" in *De libero arbitrio*, but this followed his wrenching inward journey to Christian conversion that was accompanied by a "paradigm shift" in his understanding of moral agency. Recall Augustine's fascinating account in Bk. VIII (chapters 5-12) of his *Confessions*, as he struggles to cast off his all too familiar and comfortable vices. Augustine's account is in three stages. (Reilly, 1979b) In the first, Augustine views himself in the Manichean predicament of being caught in the throes of "two wills."

> The enemy (viz. Satan) had control of my will, and out of it he fashioned a chain and fettered me with it. For in truth lust is made out of a perverse will, and when lust is served it becomes habit, and when habit is not resisted it become a necessity. . . . A new will which had begun within me, to wish freely to worship you and find joy in you, o God, the sole delight, was not yet able to overcome that prior [will]. (Augustine, 1960:188-89; Bk. VIII.5)

At this point, Augustine does not think himself then able to break the force of lustful habit; yet, echoing Aristotle, he notes that he nevertheless is responsible for the hold his habit has on him: "For the law of sin is force of habit, whereby the mind is dragged along and held fast, even against its will, but deservedly so, since it was by its will that it slipped into the habit." (Augustine, 1960:190; Bk. VIII.5)

In the second stage, Augustine begins to acknowledge his weakness as his own, as due to a defect in his current will, as when he writes:

> As for me, when I deliberated upon serving the Lord my God as I had long planned to, it was I myself who willed it and I myself who did not will it. It was I myself, I neither willed it completely nor did I refrain completely from willing it. . . . Therefore, I was at war with myself and I was laid waste by myself. (Augustine, 1960:197-98; Bk. VIII.10)

To be sure, Augustine goes on to reiterate the earlier view that it is "sin," not his (spiritual) "self" that is the culprit, but the movement from "two wills" at work to one of "incomplete willing" is quite significant for it paves the way for him to see, in the final stage of his account, that he had not yet *really* made the choice to renounce his vices. Finally, through a flood of tears, Augustine cries out, "How long, how long? Tomorrow and tomorrow? Why not now? Why not in this very hour an end to my uncleanness?" (Augustine, 1960: 202; Bk. VIII.12) No longer of the mind, "Give me chastity and continence, but not yet," Augustine is inspired to pick up and read a passage from scripture that puts an end to his doubts and struggles. And, while it might be said that his conversion was the work of God, Augustine later pinpoints the plight of the morally weak.

> But since 'the flesh lusts against the spirit and the spirit against the flesh,' so that they do not do what they wish, do they all fall down to what they are able to take, and are they satisfied with that? Is that because they are unable to do what they do not desire with sufficient strength to accomplish? (Augustine, 1960:251; Bk. X.23)

If one focuses narrowly on continually competing desires to do one thing or another, there may seem to be "two wills" at work; but the challenge is to resolve to make a determined-preference for one's "better" desire to be one's will. The capacity to make such preferences or judgments and to resolve to act upon them is the capacity of "free choice of the will," which Augustine introduces to Western culture in *De libero arbitrio*.[5] There, Augustine comments to Evodius:

> We have clearly and carefully distinguished between two sorts of things—eternal and temporal; and in turn between two sorts of human beings—those who pursue and love eternal things and those who pursue and love temporal things. We have determined that the choice to follow and embrace one or the other lies with the will, and that only the will can depose the mind from its stronghold of power and deprive it of right order. (Augustine, 1993:27; Bk I. 16)

Augustine seemingly adopts here the Platonic view that the human mind is a superior power to the human body and so it retains the prerogative of either choosing to act upon bodily desires or to refrain from doing so. And, even if one is not able to become fully righteous without divine assistance, is one doing what one can to resist temptations and to seek such assistance?

As Harry Frankfurt (1971) eloquently made clear, "free will" involves that capacity to make and to act upon "second-order desires" or what Richard Jeffrey (1974) terms "higher order preferences." Let us understand Augustine's two sorts of human beings as follows. Each has first-order preferences of the type "A pref B, Cr" meaning, "On the basis of some (e.g., temporal) criterion of act-evaluation, Cr, S prefers Aing to Bing;" and each has first-order preferences of the type "B pref A, Cr*" meaning, "On the basis of some (e.g., eternal) criterion of act-evaluation, Cr*, S prefers Bing to Aing." Second-order preferences of the form "(B pref A, Cr*) pref (A pref B, Cr)" would then mean that one prefers preferring Bing to Aing on the basis of Cr* more than Aing to Bing on the basis of Cr; or one's second order preference might be otherwise. What is crucial is one's willful intentionality: what is it that one *really prefers* oneself doing? Can one really escape this issue and one's responsibility for addressing it and for the conduct that results?

Among the most dramatic and well-known depictions of human freedom in recent Western philosophical literature are those in treatises and works of fiction offered by Jean-Paul Sartre, who provides a summary view in his oft-reprinted lecture, "Existentialism is a Humanism" (1975). On Sartre's view, the human person is a conscious being and what one is conscious of is objects; however, the conscious being as subject is categorically different from the objects which one is conscious of. Objects or things have a nature or essence that is not self-defined but attributed to it by consciousness. When we reflect upon ourselves we even see ourselves as objects, but the attributed realities of ourselves as (what I call) "concrete individuals" (objects) are not identical to who we are as subjects for we have the freedom to continuously define ourselves in novel and different ways. Hence the "facticity" that characterizes one's historical self does not, for Sartre, constitute a "nature," "essence" or "identity" that must continue over time to define who one is. One is inescapably free to "transcend" whatever one's factical self might be. One's "situation," at least in some of its parameters, might be a "given" but it is not a necessary determinant of how one chooses to act and, so, define oneself in that moment of decision. Whatever situation one finds oneself in, and this includes one's historical (self-) development to that point, there are genuine choices to be made. A well-known example that Sartre deploys in his lecture is that of a former student of his who, during the Nazi occupation of France, sought out Sartre's advice on whether he should join the French resistance or stay with his mother as her sole consolation after her husband's "half-treason" and her older son's death. Such a "conflict situation," in which one is faced with quite different kinds of options, in contrast with a choice of means to a common end, may be thought of as a defining moment because one's choice will reflect a preference or priority in one's values. We are burdened with a responsibility for choices that have no "ultimate" justification but which are made not only for ourselves but for all of humanity, since we cannot deny to others the legitimacy of options that we claim for ourselves; and we have no "excuse" for thinking that we are not responsible for how we define ourselves through the choices we make. On Sartre's view, human beings are "condemned to be free." (Sartre, 1975:353)

Now let us combine the points made by Augustine and Sartre. Both thinkers reject the Aristotelian view that "free choice" emanates out of one's settled dispositions or more stable "character;" as Augustine illustrated, presuming this view leads one to deny responsibility for conduct that is willful, that is, motivated by what the agent endorses as his preferences when refraining from such an endorsement is within one's capacity. That one would have not acted as he did had he not possessed the dispositional motivations he possessed is true; and, indeed, it might be that "then and there" the motivating dispositions are a "given" and not themselves possessed by choice. This is often the case with "first-order desires" which even animals have. Still, one normally retains the capacity to act on or to refrain from acting on the dispositions that one has through one's "higher-order preferences" by which one endorses or accepts particular first-order desires as constituting one's will when one acts. It is one's "inner awareness" of this that grounds one's own sense of responsibility for what one does. What Sartre pointedly adds to Augustine's view is that for freedom to be possible, the human person cannot be conceived as having a "nature" or essential identity, as if he were an object, a thing, indeed, the human subject is no(-)thing!

One implication of the libertarian view is that one's being free and responsible is not at all about one's "outer" circumstances, one's socially constructed identity, or, even, one's self-formed dispositions. It is a matter of the purity, the clarity of one's intentionality. The *Bhagavad-Gita* provides a vivid illustration of the manner in which one's intentionality is exercised within, but not determined by, one's life-situation, one's "karma." The *Gita* opens with the warrior-king Arjuna facing a civil war with many relatives and acquaintances as his "enemies." Arjuna is forlorn at the prospect of having to battle and to kill those who he knows and respects, but Krishna, his charioteer and the Hindu God

Vishnu in disguise, encourages Arjuna to take heart and to discharge his duty as a member of the warrior caste (Kshatriyas) and, in doing so, to do what is right because it is right (what God decrees), without thought of consequences, without fear or expectation, since what is judged "mine" and "not mine" is part of one's ego-illusion. Hinduism holds that there are multiple paths to salvation, to realizing one's inner self (Atman), hence Brahman--the main ones being the way of action (*Karma Yoga*), the way of devotion or love (*Bhakti Yoga*), the way of knowledge (*Jnana Yoga*) and the way of meditation (*Raja Yoga*). What is instructive for our purposes is that, in traditional Hinduism, one's "work" and responsibilities are a function of the caste one is born into together with one's gender and family circumstance, in short "one's karma." So, no two persons have fully identical sets of duties to fulfill. But everyone has the spiritual-ethical task of renouncing attachment to the fruits of action, of forsaking ego-involvements to do God's will for its own sake and not act for the sake of what one takes to be "mine" (*my* family, *my* friends, *my* nation). So, even if one's work is a "given," how one does it and whether one progresses towards liberation or not in doing one's work is "up to" each individual.[6]

Of course, for many people today, the "life-situation" that one has—profession, social and communal ties, marriage and familial responsibilities, and so on—involve choices that have been made and they embody one's ongoing commitments that reflect current judgments of preference. That a person is married now is not determined by the fact that he or she fell in love and married (in light of particular religious and cultural norms) ten years ago; that one is an engineer now is not determined by the talents, interests, academic credentials, and job search of twenty years ago. That one is not assertive today is not determined by one's childhood shyness of yesteryear. Even if one would not be who one is today, that is, be doing what one is doing, independently of the "self" one had been, neither would it be so if one were not now *preferring* to be doing what one is doing. What we might say is that one's life-conduct embodies one's day-to-day "higher-order preferences." That one today is a married engineer who is not self-assertive accords with a matrix of value-preferences which today one freely embraces and for which today one is answerable. So, while one has no "real self" or "concrete individuality," we may say with Sartre that "…a man is no other than a series of undertakings, that he is the sum, the organization, the set of relations that constitute these undertakings." (Sartre, 1975:359)

3. Free Rational Choices

My chief aim here is to develop a clear and coherent concept of (libertarian) free will as the capacity or power to make free rational choices. More formally, an agent exercises (libertarian) free will when the agent acts on a rationally chosen "higher-order" (or "value") preference and, at those same times, has the capacity to do otherwise, that is, to act on an alternative rationally chosen value prefer-

ence. Since the choice an agent makes in exercising free will is rationally controlled, it is explainable in terms of the agent's reasons; if reason explanations
are or entail causal explanations, then free choices are causally explainable,
though not causally determined or necessitated. Compatibilists rightly emphasize that in order to hold (appropriately) an agent responsible for her actions
(choices), it must be the case that those actions (choices) be attributable to the
agent herself. Where compatibilists go wrong is in thinking that such choices
(must) emanate from one's "character" or self-formed dispositions. The task for
incompatibilists is to provide a responsibility-conferring concept of agent control that is consistent with their intuitions that free agents have the power to act
(choose) otherwise than they do.

While a number of libertarian accounts have been developed over recent
years, this is not the time to give each its due.[7] I have benefited a great deal by
studying Robert Kane's learned and profound work. Since my account is similar
to his, I will indicate here where I find limitations in his. In *The Significance of
Free Will* [1996], Kane develops a theory of "Plural Voluntary Control" that
builds upon the earlier theory of "Dual Rational Control" presented in *Free Will
and Values* [1985]. Both theories are explicated in light of situations involving
either "moral choice" or "prudential choice." On Kane's view, moral choice and
prudential choice have similar structures: each occurs in a "conflict" situation
wherein an agent must choose between acting from duty and acting from self-
interest (moral choice) or between acting from longer term (maximizing) considerations of self-interest and acting from near-term (but not maximizing) considerations of self-interest "Consider a woman on the way to an important sales
meeting who witnesses an assault or mugging in an alley. Should she stop and
call for help or press on to avoid losing a sale crucial to her career?" (Kane,
1996:126) On Kane's analysis, in such cases of conflict agents face genuine
uncertainty about what courses of action will be chosen. Kane's businesswoman
can foresee herself doing A or doing B; what she will do will not be settled until
the moment of decision. This decision itself is indeterminate since it will result
from an indeterminate effort of will. Kane presumes that in recognizing the relevance of moral considerations (Ra), she will make an effort to choose to act
morally and do A; and in recognizing the relevance of prudential considerations
(Rb), she will make an effort to do B. But these efforts are of "indeterminate
strength;" in either case, the effort to reach the decision she reaches is her effort,
and whatever decision is reached, being the indeterminate outcome of this effort,
is her decision. In a later article, Kane put the matter this way:

> The upshot is that, despite the businesswoman's diminished control over *each*
> option considered separately, due to her conflict in her will, she nevertheless
> has what I call *plural voluntary control* over the two options *as a set*. . . . Hav-
> ing whichever of the options you will or most want, when you will to do so, for
> the reasons you will to do so, without being coerced or compelled in doing so.
> And the businesswoman . . . has this power, because whichever of the options
> she chooses . . . will be *endorsed* by her as what she wills or most wants to do
> at the moment when she chooses it. (Kane, 1999:238-39)

The main limitations of Kane's approach are three. First, it restricts "dual rational control" to "conflict situations" requiring "indeterminate efforts of will" to resolve indecision; however, we make free rational choices everyday that do not bear these characteristics. Second, what Kane refers to as *"arbitria voluntatis"* is the freedom to "arbiter" one's life, especially in circumstances wherein one might be "of two minds" on what to do based upon two quite different and incommensurable sets of considerations; however, I take issue with Kane in his characterization of the businesswoman's choice as "self-forming," meaning that the value-priority reflected in her choice becomes an element of her ongoing identity or partly forms her character. Sometimes one's "momentous" decisions are self-forming. On the other hand, if the businesswoman's decision were only that on *this* occasion she prefers acting on one of the competing criteria of act-evaluation over the other, she would not be committing herself to deciding similarly on future occasions; she need not recognize the good reason for which she acts now as constituting a compelling reason in the future. Indeed, for most agents most of the time, choices between alternative courses of action supported by good reasons do not exhibit, or get integrated into, a uniform character. Finally, "efforts of will" usually are efforts to be resolute in carrying out already made decisions about what one thinks it is best to do; such efforts are required to prevent "backsliding" or "weakness of will." It is one thing to ask, "What should I do?" and quite another to determine, "What shall I do?" We might say that moral (or prudential) conflict often challenges the agent to resist temptation and to make the choice sanctioned by moral (or maximally prudential) considerations. S could deliberate with the intention of resolving indecision about which course of action is best (for her to do here and now) or S could intend to resolve indecision about how she will act here and now on the basis of her values; but acting on either of these intentions, it seems to me, does not require (and normally is not accompanied by) "indeterminate efforts of will."[8]

A convenient point of departure for developing an alternative account of free rational choice is Donald Davidson's article, "How is Weakness of Will Possible?" (1980)[9] There Davidson draws attention to how practical reasoning in conflict situations may be compared to reasoning from probabilistic evidence. In the latter case, Davidson follows Hempel in denying that we can reason from the premises (a) "If the barometer falls, it almost certainly will rain" and (b) "The barometer is falling" to the conclusion (c), "It almost certainly will rain," since at the same time one be equally justified in arguing from the premises (a*) "Red skies at night, it almost certainly will not rain" and (b*) "The sky is red tonight" to the conclusion (c*), "It almost certainly will not rain." As Davidson remarks, the minor premises each "probabilizes, i.e., provides *prima facie* evidence for, a competing prediction about whether it will rain. Taking the premises together as constituting all the available evidence, e, we cannot infer either that e probabilizes that it will rain or that it will not rain. We may say that in this case one has *a* good reason for thinking that it will rain and *a* good reason for thinking that it will not rain, but not that one has *good reason* to believe that it will rain or to believe that it will not.

Now consider a Davidsonian species of practical reasoning.

P1 pf (A is better than B, A is a refraining from adultery and B is an act of adultery, Ra)

p1 A is a refraining from adultery and B is an act of adultery

C1 pf (A is better than B, P1 and p1).

An alternative judgment may also be arrived at:

P2 pf (B is better than A, B is a pursuing of pleasure and A is a refraining from pursing pleasure, Rb)

p2 B is a pursuing of pleasure and A is a refraining from pleasure

C2 pf (B is better than A, P2 and p2).

A judgment of particular interest is:

C3 pf (A is better than B, e [P1, p1 and P2, p2]).

Davidson's well known view is that there is no "logical conflict" between the various judgments to which one deliberates, e.g., between C1 and C2 or between C3 and either C1 or C2 since such judgments are conditioned by different sets of considerations, and, hence, each are *prima facie*. Moreover, since intentional actions stem from unconditional judgments of the form:

C4 A is better than B (or, "I shall do B!")

there can be no logical contradiction between an action and its basis and the judgments of practical reason. What Davidson intends is the possibility that one who judges (C3), "It is better to refrain from committing adultery, all things considered," may yet make the unconditional judgment (C4), "It is better to refrain from adultery [here and now]," or the unconditional judgment (C4*) "It is better not to refrain from adultery [here and now]." One's choice is represented in the unconditional judgment which may or not be in accord with one's "all things considered" comparative assessment (C3). Yet, Davidson observes:

> Carnap and Hempel have argued that there is a principle which is no part of the logic of inductive (or statistical) reasoning, but is a directive the rational man will accept. It is the requirement of total evidence for inductive reasoning: give your credence to the hypothesis supported by all available relevant evidence. There is, I suggest, an analogous principle the rational man will accept in applying practical reasoning: perform the action judged best on the basis of all available relevant reasons. It would be appropriate to call this the principle of continence. (Davidson, 1980:41)

Recall that in Davidson's example of probabilistic reasoning, one should infer neither pf(~Ra, e) nor pf(Ra, e); that is, neither conclusion is rationally warranted by the evidence on hand. What then about the comparable judgments C3 and C3*? Davidson does remark:

> of course [C3] does not follow from anything that went before, but in this respect moral reasoning seems no worse off than predicting the weather. In neither case do we know a general formula for computing how far or whether a

conjunction of evidence statements supports a conclusion from how far or
whether each conjunct supports it. (Davidson, 1980:38-39)

But whereas the weatherman can get by with the "prediction" of a "50% chance
of rain," the agent who faces a moral or prudential choice must decide one way
or the other. Given S's reasons C1 and C2 what then is it *reasonable* for S to
choose to do?

We should note first this crucial difference between making an inference to
the truth or falsity of an empirical proposition and making an "all things considered" practical judgment: while the single unambiguous criterion of "truth"
theoretically might allow for a completely systematic evaluation of all putative
evidence for the truth of empirical propositions, there is no similar, available
criterion that allows for such an evaluation of all reasons for acting. There is no
agreed upon measure by virtue of which, for example, the reasons for which any
act is morally good can be weighed rationally against the reasons for which any
competing act is prudentially good. If there were THE GOOD, then a comparison of various "species of good" might be possible. The fact is, however, there
is yet not available a persuasive account of such a measure; and, even if it were
available to the wise person, it would appear extraordinary if its possession were
a necessary condition for acting reasonably or rationally in any ordinary sense.
As things stand, there are several fundamental criteria of act-evaluation: the
moral, the prudential, the religious, the familial, and so on. The number of such
criteria and their relative priority will vary from person to person. It should be
recognized that there is a good deal of overlap among these fundamental types
of considerations, and also that certain general principles might be agreed upon
that bear on the relative weight of considerations of different types (e.g., that a
significant consideration relative to one type should always outweigh an insignificant consideration of the same type and should nearly always outweigh an
insignificant consideration of another type). Nevertheless, we all face situations
in which highly significant considerations of one type are at odds with highly
significant considerations of an alternative type. At this juncture the issue is settled by one's determining the relative priority or *importance for oneself at that
time* of the competing criteria of act-evaluation. These preferences are not one-
way rational.

Following Davidson's lead, it appears that S may judge either

C3 pf (It is better to do A than B, e) or

C3* pf (It is better to do B than A, e)

on the basis of which he should make the respective decision, i.e.,

C4 "I shall do A" or

C4* "I shall do B."

If practical decisions are based on all things considered preferential judgments
(C3's) then they may be rendered as,

C5 "All things considered, I shall do A (rather than B)."

Since C5 is an imperative rather an indicative statement, it expresses an all
things considered preference although it does not purport to represent a judg-

ment the truth of which is believed on the basis of available evidence or reasons for acting. Such "all things considered preferences" represent agents' choices and, hence, are appropriate grounds of intentional action as are judgments of the form "I shall do A" which agents might make without any consideration (let alone assessment) of reasons for acting or make on the basis of some reasons but not all, as on *prima facie* preferences such as C1 or C2.

What does it mean for choices to be "rational" or for one to "choose reasonably?" Consider this schema:

reason for believing
q is a reason for believing p iff q provides evidence for p's being the case.

reason for choosing
R(a) is a reason to choose to A iff R represents some want (end) that a rational agent might possess which successfully Aing would attain.

a good reason for believing
q is a good reason for believing p iff on the basis of q it is likely that p is the case.

a good reason for choosing
R(a) is a good reason to choose to A iff on the basis of R(a) and in light of a fundamental criterion of act evaluation, Cr, A is a desirable way to achieve the ends encompassed by Cr.

good reason for believing
S has good reason for believing p iff S believes p on the basis of q, has no reason to believe not-q, and recognizes q to be a good reason to believe p.

good reason for choosing
R(a) is good reason for S to choose to A iff R(a) is a good reason to A, Cr (for which he does A) and it is not the case both that S would judge Cr* to be more important to him in that situation and that S believes R(b) is a good reason to B, Cr*.

decisive reason for believing
q is a decisive reason for S's believing p iff S has good reason to believe q and q implies that there is high probability that p is the case.

decisive reason for choosing
R(a) is a decisive reason for S to choose A iff R(a) is good reason to A, Cr (for which she chooses to A) and S judges that Cr overrides any other criterion of act-evaluation for situations of this type.

doxastic warrant
S is warranted in his believing p iff S has a decisive reason, q, for believing p and there is no good reason for not believing q.

practical warrant
S is warranted in her choosing to do A iff S has a decisive reason for choosing to A, Cr and there is no moral criterion that overrides Cr for the situations S is in.

In light of this characterization of "choosing for good reason" or "choosing reasonably," the agent who makes the choice C4 based upon the preferential judgment, C3, chooses reasonably. The agent who holds the preferential judgment, C3, but makes the decision C4* does not choose reasonably, i.e., with good reason. A weaker sense of "rational choice" is depicted by the notion of choosing "for *a* good reason." According to this conception, an agent who judges C1 or C2 would have a good reason to make decisions C4 or C4* respectfully. Agent S who holds both C1 and C2 therefore exercises "dual rationality" in the weak sense in deciding C4 or C4*, for whichever decision she arrives at is made for a good reason. However this is not sufficient to establish that the choice is "free" in the libertarian sense of being "dual controlled." What this requires is that S's decision be supported by some "higher level" preference (e.g., C3 or C3*) and that she could have formed an effective "higher level preference" supporting the alternative decision.

   If we recast Davidsonian practical judgments in the terminology of preferences we have:

C1 and C2 respectively:	A pref B, Cr B pref A, Cr*
C3	(A pref B, Cr) pref (B pref A, Cr*)
C3*	(B pref A, Cr*) pref (A pref B, Cr)
C4 ("I shall do A [not B]!")	A pref B
C4* ("I shall do B [not A]!")	B pref A

In light of all this, I wish to reiterate why Kane's analysis of free will in terms of "efforts of will" is misguided. For Kane, "moral choice" is said to involve one's making *both* judgments C3 and C3* and, so, needing to resolve that lack of resolution by an "effort of will" in deciding on either C4 or C4*. This sort of conflict is relatively rare and certainly does not exhaust the class of situations in which one exercises "free rational choice." It is much more common that situations of "moral choice" involve one or both of the following challenges. The first is to decide which second-order preference, C3 or C3*, to make; that is, which action for which one has "good reason" for choosing does one consider to be supported by the better reason? It is this that resolves "indecision" in determining what one *rationally* should do. If one is committed to doing the moral thing over the prudent thing, then one will judge the "better" action to be the "morally responsible" action. The second challenge is to be resolute in doing that act which one takes oneself as having the better reason to do, that is to say, to make the decision, say C4, that accords with one's second-order preference, say C3. This is what may well require an "effort of will," it seems to me. There are two scenarios where the effort is unsuccessful. The first is *akrasia* (weakness of will) wherein one's "reason (second-order preference) is overcome by desire" *against* one's will. In this case, the agent has no "higher-order preference" on the basis of which her decision is made. The second scenario is more complex. Here, the agent "wills" not to act in accordance with the higher-order preference which she recognizes as providing compelling reason for choosing otherwise. The agent in this case acts in accordance with a third-order preference such as:

(B pref A, Cr*) pref [(A pref B, Cr) pref (B pref A, Cr*)]

What this means is that the agent prefers doing, say, the more pru-
dent/pleasurable action than she prefers doing what accords with her second-
order preference to act, say, morally, rather than self-centeredly. Since, the decision to act based upon such a third-order preference is in accordance with what
the agent takes to be a good reason for choosing, this preference is "rational" in
the weaker sense noted. Since this agent, unlike the *akrates*, could have resisted
doing B by not making the third-order preference rather than the second-order
preference, C3, constitute her will, her choice is free and dual-rational.

In summary, free rational choices may be said to be those "higher-order"
preferences upon which one decides to act. These preferences are based upon
"reasons for choosing" and so are "rational;" and since one's first-order reasons
do not "determine" second-order preferences, they are "free." Simply the awareness of alternative courses of action based upon incommensurable criteria of act-
evaluation is sufficient normally to explain the capacity for "free will" in situations that require moral or prudential choice. While sometimes one may be in a
state of "indecision" prior to formulating one's higher-order preferences, often
one is not; and that one does not struggle in making such judgments need not
indicate a settled firmness of "character" (to be explained in light of SFA's).
And, of course, there are those times when "efforts of will" are required to be
resolute in doing what, on the basis of good reason, one judges to be the prefer-
able course of action. But it is not the "indeterminacy" of such efforts that underlies "free will" generally; indeed, sometimes such efforts are unsuccessful
precisely because the agent cannot choose to act counter to one's strongest desire.

Finally, it should not be inferred that simply because agents choose "rationally" that therefore they cannot be criticized for the choices they make. Obviously, if an agent chooses to ignore a person in distress, she may leave herself
open to moral criticism. The grounds for judging that an agent acts reasonably
are less stringent than the grounds for judging that an agent acts justifiably (e.g.,
with moral justification) just as the criteria for reasonable belief are less demanding than are the criteria for fully justified belief.

4. Responsibility and Selflessness

As we have noted, while it is true that in order to hold appropriately an agent
responsible for her actions (choices), it must be the case that those actions
(choices) reflect the agent's preferences, it is not correct to think that this is so
because free acts (choices) emanate from one's "character" or self-forming dispositions. It is enough that a person acts from a "higher-order preference"—a
judgment that one has (a) good reason for making, based on his or her values,
even though one may be able to make instead an alternative or competing judg-

ment for equally good reason. Often our higher-order preferences do manifest in patterns of conduct and may be said to reflect one's priorities or settled dispositions. Yet, often one acts in novel ways, due to the uniqueness of the circumstances at hand, or one acts "out of character" or, even, on a whim. It is no less true that in these latter cases, one normally acts from a freely made preference (choice) and, hence, is fully responsible for the actions that result.

A perceptive view of how freedom, reason and responsibility are linked has been drawn by Susan Wolf in *Freedom Within Reason* (1990). Wolf proposes what she calls The Reason View: "an agent is responsible if and only if the agent can do the right thing for the right reasons." (Wolf, 1990:81) On Wolf's account, one has "right reasons" in light of what she calls "the True and the Good." There appear to be four possibilities: (1) a responsible person may do the right thing for the right reasons and not be able to choose otherwise because of the perceived rightness of her reasons together with her commitment to doing what is right; (2) a responsible person may do the right thing for the right reasons and be able to choose otherwise; (3) a person may fail to do the right thing for the right reasons, but have the ability to do otherwise, that is, to have done the right thing for the right reasons; (4) a person may fail to do the right thing for the right reasons and not have the ability to do otherwise, that is, to have done the right thing for the right reasons. The Reason View, Wolf claims, is a middle way between "The Autonomy View" and the "Real Self View." According to The Autonomy View, the ability necessary for responsibility is an ability to do [choose] one thing *or* another; what is crucial here is that one could have done [chosen] otherwise. On The Real Self View, on the other hand, an agent is responsible if and only if she is able to form her actions on the basis of her values (no matter what they are or how they have been acquired).

Three problems Wolf finds with The Autonomy View are: (a) it places "responsible agents" outside of the determinates of causes and conditions; (b) it implies that one is as responsible for choices/deeds not formed by the True and the Good, including even those done against one's Reason, as for choices that are so formed; and, (c) it would deny responsibility in the case of (1) above, where we would want to praise the good person for doing the right thing, even more so if she contends that she acted from a compelling reason and "could not (have brought herself to) have done/chosen otherwise." I think that the Autonomy View can avoid the first problem by analyzing reasons for acting as non-necessitating ("indeterminate") causes; and, as for the second, the sense of "responsible" I take to be relevant in this context is to be "answerable" or "accountable" *for* one's choices. Yes, there is a difference in being responsible *in* one's choices or in the performance of one's duties, which implies that one has performed one's duties well, and being responsible *for* one's choices or for the performance or lack thereof of one's duties. In terms of accountability, the person who does not do what is right for the right reasons can be just as "responsible" as the person who does so act. Below, I will show how the view of rational free choices accounts for agents being responsible for actions in circumstances in which they "could not have chosen (and acted) otherwise."

A problem with The Real Self View, as Wolf notes, is that, due to say a depraved childhood, a person's values may be skewed in a way that does not enable her to do the right thing for the right reasons; such a person yet can form her actions on the basis of her values as much as can a person whose values are formed by the True and the Good, but she cannot be thought to be similarly responsible when she fails to do what is right for the right reasons. (Wolf, 1990:68-89) In these cases, presumably, the agent's wayward actions are not done in accordance with higher-order preferences that are freely and rationally chosen.

Wolf's analysis can be adapted to our preceding account of free rational choices with two caveats. First, it is difficult to see how The Reason View can be committed to one's real self being the bearer of one's values, based on the True and the Good, as Wolf maintains (Wolf, 1990:75), for if this were so, it would not accommodate Wolf's interesting distinctions between one who has the ability to do what is right for the right reasons and can do no other and one who has the ability to do what is right for the right reasons and can do or does otherwise. How can one be a responsible "real self agent" while acting *against* the good (or compelling) reasons he has for doing the right thing? If he acts on the basis of rationally weaker motives, how is it to be maintained that in addition to knowing the right reasons on the basis of which he should act that he also, at the time he acts, has the power to convert his knowledge into action? [That The Autonomy View maintains this possibility is an important point of criticism by Wolf.] Also, Wolf speaks consistently in terms of one's values rather than in terms of one's character, and, it seems to me, one's values can be based on one's reasons that reflect the True and the Good in multiple configurations, meaning that there need not be an enduring self configured in some particular way in order for one to be a responsible agent. Furthermore, as Kane has emphasized, as well as Sartre, it might be that one's values are not all commensurable or congruent with one another and thus "conflict situations" arise that are not settled in some one way as a result of the person being the person he has been. So, for our purposes, let us say that the middle way forward is one in which a responsible agent is one who intentionally acts in accordance with freely and rationally chosen higher-order preferences. The second caveat, then, is that for Wolf, "right reasons" tend to be "justifying reasons" and to act in light of the True and the Good is to act with appropriate justification or warrant. For our purposes, we can adopt Wolf's perspective but be less demanding on the warrant provided by the agent's reasons for acting; in short, an appropriate criterion for one choosing rationally is that one has "good reason" for choosing as one does rather than that one is "justified" in her choosing as she does. (See above schema, p.109)

As we have seen, one's deliberations can proceed along parallel chains of reasoning. Let us revisit Kane's businesswoman with both the following notions in mind.

good reason for choosing: R(a) is good reason for S to choose A iff R(a) is a good reason to A, Cr and it is not the case both that S judges

Cr* to be more important to him in the situation and S believes (Rb) is good reason to B, Cr*.

.

decisive reason for choosing: R(a) is a decisive reason for S to choose A iff R(a) is good reason to A, Cr and S judges that Cr overrides any other criterion of act-evaluation for situations of this type.

Kane's businesswoman (S) has good reason for choosing to render immediate aid to the assault victim, R(a), Cr, where Cr represents doing what compassion requires; and she has good reason for choosing to attend the sales meeting, R(b), Cr*, where Cr* represents doing what career success requires. In this situation, that S possesses R(a) and R(b) means that she has conflicting first-order wants or preferences. "Free will" is the capacity to choose to make higher-order judgments of preference as to which first-order preferences shall constitute one's will. From this perspective, we may say that practical indecision such as the businesswoman's is settled by one's determining the relative priority or importance for oneself of the competing criteria of act evaluation. In sum, S's decision to A on the basis of a second-order judgment [(A pref B, Cr) pref (B pref A, Cr*)] is a decision to act in accordance with a "free choice of the will" since S could have made an alternative second-order judgment [(B pref A, Cr*) pref (A pref B, Cr)] her will instead. Since each second-order judgment of preference is rationally grounded in S's reasons for acting, the choice between them is not "necessitated" by the reasons (first-order wants or preferences) S has and the choice between them is "dual rational." While S does not have decisive reason for choosing otherwise than she does, since, for example, she does not hold the principle that what compassion requires always overrides what professional success requires, she does embrace the choice she makes as "her own," as expressing "her will" then and there. She holds herself responsible, and is willing to be held accountable by others since her choice, as Kane puts it, accords with her intention to make choices rationally grounded in her values, which she succeeds in doing.

In sum, "dual rational control" most often is exercised by agents in situations where they have "(a) good reason" to choose more than one course of action. Furthermore, I have claimed, such choices need not reflect one's settled character or self-formed dispositions; nor need they be self-forming or defining of one's character from that point onwards. What I now wish to clarify is how the foregoing representation of free rational choices coheres with Wolf's "Reason View" in offering a middle way between the accounts of responsibility based on the "Real Self View" and on the "Autonomy View."

Recall that Wolf's main objection against the Autonomy View is that it denies that one is responsible for doing the right thing for the right reasons when, at that time, one is not able to choose otherwise because of the perceived rightness of her actions together with her commitment to doing what is right. Typically such choices may be *represented* as a higher order preference of the form [(A pref B, Cr) pref (B pref A, Cr*)]; but the person who has unwavering com-

mitment to doing what is right, based on Cr, will see herself as having little or
no reason for overriding that judgment and, so, in words that echo Euripides'
Medea, for "seeing the better course but choosing the worse." The notion here
of having "little or no" choice is parallel to that which characterizes stereotypi-
cal situations of coercion, e.g., "Your money or your life." Might we not appropriately say that, in both cases, the agent "could not have (brought herself to
have) chosen otherwise"—just because it would have been so irrational for her
to make a deliberate choice contrary to the option supported by the clear pre-
dominance of her rational considerations? I think it might well be true of one
and the same agent that: (1) he acts out of free choice of the will, in that he acts
from a freely and rationally formed value-preference, and (2) therefore he acts
responsibly, but (3) he could not have (brought himself to have) acted otherwise
than he did. The Autonomy View, on Wolf's account, is wrong since it presumes that a person is responsible only for those acts which the person at the
time could have chosen not to perform, whereas, on the wider view being advanced here, one is responsible for all actions done in accordance with one's
(freely and rationally chosen) higher-order preferences. Furthermore, this line
of analysis can be extended to agents who are carrying out tasks associated with
their life-routines, since these routines reflect a myriad of value-preferences
which are embraced as being "rationally and freely formed." In the midst of
one's life-routines, one continually acts in ways that accord with one's higher-
order preferences and, in the (non-negligent) absence of any good reason to act
otherwise, it might be true that one could not have (brought oneself to have)
acted otherwise, since one would have had no real reason for doing so. Yet, such
acts are acts for which one is responsible.

According to Wolf, as we have noted, "an agent is responsible if and only if
the agent can do the right thing for the right reasons." Is this view warranted? I
think it can be understood in a way that is defensible. First, we need to keep in
mind that what makes an agent responsible *in* her conduct is that she does the
right thing for the right reasons; but, what makes her responsible *for* her conduct
is that she intentionally acts in accordance with a freely and rationally chosen
higher-order preference. While, as we have seen, Wolf is correct in holding that
an agent is responsible for doing what is right for the right reasons even if she
lacks, then and there, the ability to (bring herself to) act otherwise, as the
Autonomy View requires, it is also true that a person who fails to do the right
thing for the right reasons might be responsible for his failure even though he,
then and there, could not have brought himself to have acted otherwise. The
person who fails to do what is right for the right reasons, just as the agent who
does what is right for the right reasons, might well be acting in accordance with
a freely and rationally chosen higher-order preference; this is what makes
agents' actions expressions of "free will," and this provides the grounds for
holding agents responsible for their actions. It well may be, as we often think it
is, that the consistently righteously-motivated person *cultivates* her character in
light of the True and the Good whereas the person who all too frequently fails to
act rightly for the right reasons has become habituated by his acting in accor-

dance with higher-order preferences which, while rational, are not warranted. Nevertheless, both the righteous person and, say, the egoist might wholeheartedly be committed to their value preferences and, over time, see "little or no" reason to act contrary to them. Still, the non-righteous among us typically can bring ourselves to embrace warranted higher-order preferences, if they have good reason to reconsider their life-orientation, and so, perhaps over time, consistently do the right thing for the right reason. If we take "can do the right thing for the right reason" to include not only what one is able to do then and there (as the Autonomy View insists) but also what one reasonably can bring oneself to do in similar situations in the future, then we can agree with Wolf's specification of the Reason View of agent-responsibility.

To recapitulate, free choice of the will is the capacity to rationally embrace one or another "higher-order preference" and, I have argued, one is responsible for those actions which one does in accordance with a rationally chosen higher-order preference. To use a Sartrean notion, a person's will is a dynamic ensemble of higher-order preferences, not all congruent or even consistent with one another; and, often, when one acts in accordance with one's "higher-order preference" one is aware of having reason for choosing to act on an alternative preference instead. On this view, a person, as practical agent, does not possess an enduring "self" or a determinate "character" which is the basis of one's accountability. Even if one acts "out of character," "on a whim" or from "moral weakness," one acts responsibly because one's act reflects a "higher-order preference" that expresses one's there-and-then values. One's choices need not reflect one's settled character or self-formed dispositions; and, they need not be self-forming or defining of one's character from that point onwards. Nevertheless, even where an agent is so committed to certain value-preferences that she sees no good reason for acting contra-wise, as long as those preferences are/were rationally chosen, and, hence are subject to rational reconsideration, then she is responsible for her actions in accordance with them.

5. Praising and Blaming

It is because people have the capacity to think critically and to order and reorder their lives that we hold people responsible for their actions not only by praising and blaming them but also by rewarding and punishing them. Being "responsible" for what one does, one may be the subject of praise or blame. In terms of Wolf's four-fold classification above, responsible agents who do what is right for the right reasons are appropriate subjects of praise; whereas responsible agents who fail to do what is right or who fail to do what is right for the right reasons are appropriate subjects of blame. For what purposes should people be praised or blamed? And, what should be one's attitude towards persons who are not responsible for not doing what is right for the right reasons? Let's consider these questions in light of the ethics of compassion.

In Chapter III, we saw that "acting rightly" means not causing beings to suffer unnecessarily and protecting beings from or relieving beings of unnecessary suffering. To praise someone for doing what is right should not be done in a manner that might tend to boost his or her "ego" since, in acting compassionately, one acts "selflessly" and any movement to foster ego-gratification would be incongruous for one whose aspiration is to free all beings from suffering. Nevertheless, it is a beneficial practice (of "sympathetic joy") to share in another's compassionate intentionality in order to affirm the other's good-heartedness and support the good that is done. With regard to someone who fails to do the right thing for the right reasons, but could have done so, it is important to keep in mind that such an agent realizes that he or she did not act for the best of reasons (for otherwise, he or she would not have had the ability to do what is right for the right reasons). Furthermore, such an agent does not have a "defective character" that explains why he or she did not do the right thing for the right reasons; for, if it were the agent's "character" that were to explain his or her choice, then, again, he or she would not have had the ability to do what is right for the right reasons. For these considerations, "blame" should not be thought of in terms of "condemnation" of the person. The responsible person who fails to do what is right for the right reasons, should acknowledge the "failure" but not incur thereby a disheartening attitude towards one's being, since this would reinforce the human tendencies either to see oneself as "bad" (and hence not prone to be "good') or to disassociate oneself from the motive(s) of "bad" conduct and so deny one's being responsible, when one is, for not doing what is right for the right reasons (as Augustine illustrated). Since a responsible person who fails to do the right thing for the right reasons is aware of this "failure" and, hence, already "blames himself," the compassionate response is to gently encourage, inspire and assist him or her to choose to do what is right for the right reasons; and the best "teaching" for this is the example of one's own perseverance and commitment in doing what is right for the right reasons rather than words of anger or, even, words of mild-tempered "correction." One's *being* compassionate (or acting compassionately) towards someone who fails to do the right thing for the right reason provides rich inspiration for him or her not to so choose in the future.

The remaining type of case is where someone who lacks the ability to do the right thing for the right reason fails to do so. Obviously there are two general kinds of explanations for this inability; in Wolf's terms, they are the inability "to *know* what is in accordance with the True and the Good" and the inability of *execution*, "to convert one's knowledge into action." (Wolf, 1990:88) Wolf says of the agent who is incapable of genuine friendship, unable to have different and better values and to change herself in accordance with the True and the Good, that she is "to be pitied rather than blamed." (Wolf, 1990:86) Of course, there are degrees of abilities and inabilities; but, I suggest, most people have the capacities to change "in accordance with the True and the Good" over time, if not at the moment. In Chapter III, we discussed the "Love Commandment" and whether it makes sense to "command" people to love and we settled on the notion that people could assume the commitment to act lovingly; and, similarly, people who have been quite thoughtless and unaware of the values and proprieties of friendship, may still begin to understand and appropriate them. Again, this can be fostered by others being their friends, by modeling the conduct that exhibits the True and the Good (of friendship). But to see how a friendless person suffers, and to respond to her suffering, is not to find her pitiable but deserving of compassion.

If persons are not concrete individuals with inherited or acquired "natures," then there is nothing about a person as such that warrants one's condemnation. The *paramita* of patience or inclusiveness enables one to be in situations with a mind clear of expectations and fears and, in not expecting anything, one is not disturbed by or judgmental about what occurs; hence, there is no self-concerned reason to be angry with or blaming of another. Even if one thinks it appropriate to judge actions but not persons, it does not follow that one is warranted in blaming *persons* for the actions/choices they make; what is owed wrongdoers, as it were, is understanding, concern and support to strengthen them to do what is right for the right reasons. In Buddhist practice there is a prayer of supplication to Avalokiteshvara, the Bodhisattva of Compassion, which runs:

> *Should even the myriad beings of the*
> *Three Realms without exception*
> *Become angry at us, humiliate,*
> *Criticize, threaten or even kill us,*
> *We seek your blessings to complete the*
> *Perfection of patience not to be distraught,*
> *But to work for their benefit*
> *In response to their harm.*

Still, one might respond, is it not often appropriate to hold persons *accountable* who knowingly fail to do the right thing for the right reasons? What of the situation of Kant's judge, discussed in Chapter I? Even though "punishment" is the infliction of a suffering (Fingarette, 1977), is not punishment of criminal offenders justified and, furthermore, how can they be punished without being condemned?

The first point to keep in mind is that "legal responsibility" attaches to the *de facto* intentionality of the defendant who does or causes a prohibited harm rather than to the defendant as a person; we punish people for what they criminally (will to) do, not for who they are. There is no need, then, for the criminal today to have the *mens rea* ("guilty mind" or "criminal intentionality" or motivations) with which yesterday he did a prohibited act for him today to be found to legally responsible and, consequently, to face "punishment" tomorrow. In other words, "punishment" does not require the assumption of a "real self" as the subject of punishment.

Secondly, we should remember that compassion bids one not to cause one to suffer *unnecessarily*, meaning in a way not necessary for that being's own good. In the *Georgius* (400c-d), Plato drew an analogy between the functions of medicine and "legal justice:" just as the physician, sometimes through surgery or other painful remedies, cures one of physical disease and restores one to health, so too the judge, through appropriate "sentencing," annuls the defendant's unjust intentionality and restores him to the community. Of course, our policies and practices of incarceration might not have this outcome (or aim); but the point is that the rationale of punishment can be conceived in terms of "rectifying" a criminal intentionality much like a parent's punishment of a child is to "teach a lesson" that will well serve the child, be conducive to its well being. Moreover, within this context, the beneficial goal of protecting the community from lawlessness, that is preventing sufferings that might otherwise occur, can be addressed as well.[10]

As a case in point, consider the following episode that was discussed in correspondence by the Cistercian monk, Thomas Merton, and the Zen master, D.T. Suzuki.

> There was once a great hermit in the mountains and he was attacked by robbers. But his cries aroused the other hermits in the neighborhood, and they ran together and captured the robbers. These they sent under guard to the town and the judge put them in jail. But then the brothers were very ashamed and sad because, on their account, the robbers had been turned over to the judge. They went to Abbot Poemen and told him all about it. And the elder wrote to the hermit saying: Remember who carried out the first betrayal, and you will learn the reason for the second. Unless you had first been betrayed by your own inward thoughts, you would never have ended by turning those men over to the judge. The hermit, touched by these words, got up at once and went into the city and broke open the jail, letting out the robbers and freeing them from torture. (Merton, 1968:106n)

The hermit's attachment to possessions and to self, i.e., to what he thought of as "mine," led him to "betray" the robbers, to exclude them from his compassionate concern. As Suzuki comments: "The 'great hermit' is guilty of not realizing Emptiness, that is, Innocence." Moreover, Suzuki adds, "and Abbot Poeman commits an error of applying Innocence minus Knowledge to the affairs of the world." (Merton, 1968:107) What are we to make of this? For Merton, Abbot Poeman's point is that it is not a hermit's business to send thieves to jail. But, is this the end of the matter? Suzuki raises the issue of one's responsibility to the community as well as to the individuals whom one meets. Granted that one should not be a party to torture (assuming that its harms are not minimally necessary to achieve a greater good for its subjects), or to take vengeance upon others, or, even, to be angry with others, still, should not one (also) act to protect the community from harm, if possible?

In fact, holding persons accountable respects their "dignity" and is consistent with concern for their well-being. Policies of long-tem imprisonment or harsh punishments, however, may aim to break the criminal's will and, in any case, have the effect of weakening the capacity for free rational choices that is characteristic of responsible agency. It is more humane to accept defendants for who they are, to make it clear how certain intentionalities are harmful to others' well being and to their own as well, and to work with them to adopt more mindfulness. This might require their separation from the community, in one way or another; so addressing the needs of those who manifest a willingness to harm others as well as the need of community for protection from those willing to be harmful, are mutually reinforced.

In summary, the notion of a responsible moral agent, an agent who can do the right thing for the right reason, coheres well with the notions that such agents are "free" and "selfless." Free rational choices are not consistent with The Real Self View in which one's choices reflect one's settled dispositions, character or "self-identity" rather than one's current higher-order judgments or preferences, one's reasons for acting, that are grounded in values that one then and there embraces but which need not define who one is. Moreover, one's ability to do the right thing for the right reasons is not much affected by one's life-situation or "karma," assuming that one possesses normal human capacities. Finally, given the selflessness of moral agents, one's response to those who do what is right for the right reasons or who fail to do so should not focus on praising or blaming them; rather, one should maintain an attitude of "equanimity" towards them, joyfully sympathetic with those who bestow good and fully compassionate towards those who fail to.

NOTES

1. That Mahāyāna Buddhism is thought to be based on an "ethico-metaphysical" inconsistency is a common objection. For an overview, see Beane (1974), who argues in support of the claim, "at the heart of Buddhism lies an apparent ethico-metaphysical accountability which implies an 'agent' who is accountable; yet personal experience of such an agent has not been held as philosophically admissible;" and, "there can hardly be an experience of compassion without a directly proportionate sense of unified personal agency." (Beane, 1974:441; 455-56)

2. For a perceptive treatment of the history of the freewill-determinism debate, especially in modern Western philosophy, see Kane (1985). For more recent developments and for fine bibliographies, see Kane (2002).

3. For a masterful account of "practical reason" that places Aristotle's essential insights regarding "deliberative choice" and the practical syllogism within a broader context of providing a compatibilist-causal account of intentional actions for which one is responsible, see Audi, 1989. Audi observes:

Since strongly compelled actions can be based on practical reasoning, it would be wrong to say that the agent is morally responsible for every action so based. A kind of causal responsibility is implied by an action's being based upon practical reasoning but that does not entail moral responsibility. However, it does appear that if we act freely *and* on the basis of practical reasoning, then, other things being equal, we bear greater moral responsibility. . . . The explanation of this difference is apparently that the action is both reasoned and undertaken in light of a judgment which is itself based on reasoning. This indicates a kind of endorsement of the action by the agent . . . Other things equal, the action better represents the character of the agent, or at least represents both the intellect *and* the will. (Audi, 1989:140)

Audi is correct in indicating that an action (choice) for which one is responsible involves the agent's "rational endorsement;" however, I do not think that, it turn, this is to be explained in terms of the "character" of the agent; nor can it be explained in light of Aristotelian "practical syllogisms" for these do not allow the agent to form reasoned preferences when "competing syllogisms" apply within a given situation. See Section 3 below.

4. That Aristotle's main account of weakness of will fails to account for its blameworthiness is argued in Reilly (1976).

5. For an illuminating exposition of Augustine's understanding of "free will," see Stump, 2001. Stump argues persuasively that Augustine never abandoned the account of free will presented in *De libero arbitrio*; and she shows how this account can be explicated in light of Frankfurt's concept of "second-order" desires or volitions. What complicates immensely the issue of free will for Augustine is the Pelagian controversy regarding the role of divine grace in one's willing the good; even here Stump offers a plausible way forward that is consistent with the account of free will in *De libero arbitrio*.

6. Sartre expresses the point this way:

His historical situations are variable: man may be born a slave in a pagan society or may be a feudal baron, or a proletarian. But what never vary are the necessities of being in the world, of having to labor and to die there. These limitations are neither subjective nor objective, or rather there is both a subjective and an objective aspect of them. Objective, because we meet with them everywhere and they are everywhere recognizable: and subjective because they are *lived* and are nothing if man does not live them—if, that is to say, he does not freely determine himself and his existence in relation to them. (Sartre, 1975.362)

Buddha Shakyamuni reportedly declared:

Since you are searching for understanding of self, don't ask about caste or class, riches or birth, but instead ask about heart and conduct. Look at the flames from a fire. Where does the brightness arise? From the nature of wood—and it doesn't matter what kind of wood. In the same way the bright heart of wisdom can shine from wood of every sort. It is through virtuous conduct, through loving-kindness and compassion, and through understanding of truth that one becomes noble. (Kornfield, 2008:71-72)

7. For an anthology of representative views on indeterminism and free will, see O'Connor (1995). The view closest to my own (see Reilly, 1979b) is Laura Waddell Ekstrom's "Indeterminist Free Action" (2001).

8. In fact, I believe that Kane's account of "free choice" as involving "indeterminate efforts of will" cannot explain an important class of cases, viz., cases of "weakness of will." In a forthcoming paper ("Can Libertarianism Account for Weakness of Will?"), I

argue against the coherence of the explanation of weakness of will provided in "Libertarianism and Rationality Revisited" (Kane, 1988).

9. First published in *Moral Concepts*, ed. Joel Feinberg, Oxford University Press, 1970 and reprinted with revisions in Donald Davidson (1980) to which page citations refer. This starting point might be surprising to some since Davidson is well known as a "causal theorist." Also, Frankfurt is known as a "compatibilist." Yet, I think that adopting their analyses lends added credence to the account I provide.

10. It will be recalled that Plato did not eschew capital punishment, holding in Bk. III of *The Republic*, for example, that the incurably diseased should be allowed to die and the incurably unjust should be put to death. Obviously, for Plato, a man is benefited by punishment, because his soul is benefited—in this world or the next. This is not the view I am here advocating. Rather, "punishment" or "legal justice" provides for the opportunity for the community to benefit itself *and* to benefit, "in this life," the person who has willed to harm his fellow beings.

Postscript
Joyful Living

A person is truly pure of heart when he considers all human beings as good and no created thing appears impure or defiled to him.

St. Isaac of Syria

In the world's spiritual literature, as exemplified by Augustine's *Confessions* and the *Bhagavad-Gita*, a prevalent theme is that one is called upon to transcend one's attachments to what is regarded as "me" and "mine" (i.e., to one's ordinary "self") and to purify one's heart or intentionality. What this might involve is revealed in a text from *Isaiah*.

> Wash yourselves, make yourselves clean.
> Take away the evil from your souls before my eyes!
> Cease to do evil,
>   learn to do good!
> Seek justice,
>   correct oppression,
>   defend the fatherless,
>   plead for the widow. (*Is* I: 15-17)

Committing oneself to ceasing to do evil and learning to do good does not require one to be in any particular life-situation because it is applicable to any life-situation of a human being of normal capacity. The current Dalai Lama often recounts the story of a Buddhist monk, Lopon-la, who was imprisoned in Tibet for many years—subjected to "re-education," on many occasions tortured, and harassed constantly by his guards. When asked if he was ever afraid, Lopon-la "admitted that there was one thing that had scared him: the possibility that he might lose compassion and concern for his jailers." (Dalai Lama, 1999: 102) In a similar vein, St. Seraphim of Sarov, a monk-contemporary of Peter the Great, when asked how it was possible for him to share his meager ration of bread with all the bears, wolves, lizards and snakes he encountered, replied, "There is always enough." (Forest, 1999: 94) These monks simply did not think in terms of "me" and "mine," of "self" and "other." In the words of St. Isaac of Syria: "Let mercy outweigh all else in you. Let compassion be a mirror where we may see in ourselves that likeness and that true image which belong to the Divine nature and Divine essence." (Forest: 89)

A Christian might say that by seeing in ourselves (the likeness of) the divine essence, one sees it in others as well; the Tibetan-Buddhist might say that by seeing "the lama within" one sees the self-liberating Buddha-nature in all. With reference to the Man of Innocence (the pure of heart) Merton quotes St. Paul, "Against such there is no law!" And, then adds, "He might as well have said *For* such there is no law. It works both ways—the law has for them neither advantages or disadvantages....They are 'beyond the law.'" (Merton, 1968:100) Indeed, they are "beyond the law" in that they do act because of the law or out of rational consideration of the law; rather, they act utterly naturally, spontaneously, non-reflectively, without discrimination, in purity of heart. In so being, they *are* spirit of the law; the law is not against what they do and what they do is neither for nor against the law. The Tibetan-Buddhist might speak similarly of one who has "given birth to compassion" in attaining "absolute Bodhicitta."

Our situation might well be different, if we have not attained "purity of heart" or "the realization of emptiness." We earlier discussed the propriety of the Gospel's "Love Commandment" obligating one to not only act lovingly (compassionately) but to be loving (compassionate), on the grounds that compassion is available within one's nature as a human being and can be generated or summoned. It was noted then that while *being* compassionate (spontaneously acting from compassion when and as appropriate) as a state of moral perfection might be our aspiration, our "obligation" in the "here and now" is to *decide to act* compassionately and that this might require effort in so far as we have conflicting tendencies, dispositions and priorities. So, in maintaining a pure intentionality to always act compassionately, one is in the same situation that Augustine and Arjuna found themselves—struggling with ego-centeredness and with tendencies to be attached to what is identified with one's self.[1]

Ethics of compassion, in short, are rooted in the tension between one's conceiving oneself as a concrete individual with one's "own" dispositions, desires and reasons for acting and as a being, at root, inter-connected with and concerned about others. Indeed this tension is embedded in the line of reasoning that runs:

1. As a living being, I have a will to live, prosper and avoid unnecessary suffering.
2. All living beings have a will to live, prosper and to avoid unnecessary suffering.
3. I would not wish for any living being to cause me unnecessary suffering.
4. One ought not to treat any living being as one would not wish to be treated.

5. I ought not to cause any living being to suffer unnecessarily.

The reasoning begins with the notion of oneself as *a* (particular) living being with a will for one's own happiness; but, by adopting the Golden Rule, one begins to equate others with oneself and compassion, or fellow-feeling generally, brings one to identify others and oneself. However, in so far as such an identification is not spontaneously ongoing we feel resistance to being empathetic and compassionate, distracted as we are by other concerns, interests and goals. In noticing this, we should not think that we cannot be(come) compassionate; rather, we should recognize in our "resistance" what we need to "work on," what we need to "detach" ourselves from in order to remain open and responsive to the felt needs of others. Doing this for most of us, from a practical perspective, is aided by "reminders" or "mindfulness practices" such as abiding by "precepts."[2] Of course the spirit of the law, *being* pure of heart or compassionate, supersedes *following* the letter of the law, but it is not as though one acts against the law.

Oddly, we are motivated in doing so because of the joy we experience in helping others, in feeling deeply connected with them, and in rejoicing in their happiness. The happiness we wish for ourselves is not stabilized in a life in which one pursues happiness for oneself; rather, it seems to arise most assuredly and most enduringly in the context of our love, concern and compassion for others.[3] In the words of Chogyam Trungpa:

> When a person develops real compassion, he or she is uncertain whether he is being generous to others or to himself, because compassion is environmental generosity, without direction, without "for me" and without "for them." It is filled with joy, spontaneously existing joy, constant joy in the sense of trust, in the sense that joy contains tremendous wealth, richness. (Trungpa, 2002:99)

NOTES

1. How to develop such compassion is a matter of spiritual practice and most spiritual traditions provide an array of detailed practices for serious practitioners.

2. Intermediate practices, in the Mahāyāna Buddhist tradition, involve meditations on "the four boundless qualities" of love, compassion, sympathetic joy and equanimity; two sources written for Western readers are Salzberg (2002) and Wallace (1999). A spiritual path for Christians is the "Ladder of the Beatitudes" of the Eastern Orthodox tradition, nicely presented in Forest (1999).

3. Often one hears how "fortunate" it is that sexual intercourse is so pleasant, for otherwise the race might not survive! Similarly, that altruistic attitudes like "kindness," "forgiveness," "cooperation," and "compassion," really do make people "feel good" about themselves is fortunate indeed given the benefits of living in community.

Works Cited

Adkins, A.W.H. 1960. *Merit and Responsibility*. Oxford: The Clarendon Press.

Aitken, Robert. 1984. *The Mind of Clover: essays in Zen Buddhist ethics*. New York: North Point Press.

Allinson, Robert E. 1985. "The Confucian Golden Rule: A Negative Formulation." *Journal of Chinese Philosophy*. Vol. 12, 305-315.

_____. 1992. "The Golden Rule as the Core Value in Confucianism & Christianity: Ethical Similarities and Differences." *Asian Philosophy*. Vol. 2.2, 173-85.

Aquinas, St. Thomas. 1920. *Summa Theologica*. Trans. Fathers of the English Dominican Province. London: Burns, Oates & Washbourne, Ltd.

Aristotle. 1941a. *De Anima*. Trans. J.A. Smith. *The Basic Works of Aristotle*. Ed. Richard McKeon. New York: Random House.

_____. 1941b. *Ethica Nicomachea*. Trans. W.D. Ross. *The Basic Works of Aristotle*. Ed. Richard McKeon. New York: Random House.

_____. 1941c. *Rhetorica*. Trans. W. Rhys Roberts. *The Basic Works of Aristotle*. Ed. Richard McKeon. New York: Random House.

_____. 1947. *Politics*. Trans. Benjamin Jowett. *Introduction to Aristotle*, Ed. Richard McKeon, New York: Random House.

Audi, Robert. 1973. "Intending." *Journal of Philosophy*, 70, 387-403.

_____. 1989. *Practical Reasoning*. London & New York: Routledge.

Augustine. 1960. *The Confessions*. Trans. John K. Ryan. Garden City, NY: Doubleday (Image Books).

_____. 1993. *On Free Choice of the Will*. Trans. Thomas Williams. Indianapolis & Cambridge: Hackett Publishing Company.

Barad, Judith. 2007. "The Understanding and Experience of Compassion: Aquinas and the Dalai Lama." *Buddhist Christian Studies*, 27:11-29.

Baron, Marcia W. 1995. *Kantian Ethics Almost Without Apology*. Ithaca and London: Cornell University Press.

Beane, Wendell C. 1974. "Buddhist Causality and Compassion." *Religious Studies*, X:441-56.

Bernard of Clairvaux. 1987. "On Conversion," XVII.31. *Bernard of Clairvaux: Selected Works*. Trans. G.R. Evans, New York: Paulist Press: 90-91.

Bhagavad Gītā. 1986. Trans. Barbara Stoler Miller. New York: Bantam Books.

127

Blum, Lawrence A. 1980a. "Compassion." *Explaining Emotions*, 507-17. Ed. Amelie Oksenberg Rorty. Berkeley: University of California Press, 1980.

_____. 1980b. *Friendship, Altruism and Morality.* London & Boston: Routledge & Kegan Paul.

Bonaventure. 1995. *Collations on the Ten Commandments.* Ed. and Trans. Paul Spaeth. St. Bonaventure University Press.

Brown, Lee M. 1996. "Compassion and Societal Well-being." *Pacific Philosophical Quarterly*, 77, 216-24.

Buddha, Shakymuni. 1991. *Sammaditthi Sutta (Majjhima Nikaya 9)*, 15-17. In *The Wheel Publication* No. 377/379. Trans. Bhikkhu Nanamoli. Ed. Bhikkhu Bodhi. Kandy, Sri Lanka: Buddhist Publication Society. web.mit.edu/stclair/www/sammaditthi.html.

_____. 2006. *Early Buddhist Discourses,* Ed. and Trans. by John J. Holder. Indianapolis: Hackett Publishing Co.

Carr, Brain. 1996. "Pity and Compassion as Social Virtues." *Philosophy*, 74, 411-429.

Cartwright, David E. 1982. "Compassion." Zeit der Emte; Studien zim Stand Schopenhauer-Forschung; Festscrift feur Arthur Heubscher zum 85. Geburtstag. 60-69.

_____. 1988. "Schopenhauer's Compassion and Nietzsche's Pity." *Schopenhauer-Jahrbuch*, 69, 557-67.

Chödrön, Pema. 1991. *The Wisdom of No Escape.* Boston: Shambhala Publications.

Confucius. 1861. *Analects.* Trans. James Legge. *The Chinese Classics*, Vol. I, 137-354. Safety Harbor, FL: Simon Publications.

Dalai Lama (aka Tenzin Gyatso). 1996. *The Good Heart.* Boston: Wisdom Publications.

_____. 1999. *Ethics for a New Millennium.* New York: Riverhead Books (Penguin Putnam).

_____. 2000. *The Meaning of Life*, Rev. ed. Trans. and Ed. by Jeffrey Hopkins. Boston: Wisdom Publications.

_____. 2001. *An Open Heart: Practicing Compassion in Everyday Life.* Ed. Nicholas Vreeland. Boston, New York & London: Little, Brown and Company.

_____. 2002. *How to Practice: The Way to a Meaningful Life.* Trans. and Ed. Jeffrey Hopkins. New York & London: Pocket Books (Simon & Schuster).

Davidson, Donald. 1980. *Essays on Actions and Events.* Oxford: Clarendon Press.

Drengston, Alan R. 1981. "Compassion and Transcendence of Duty and Inclination." *Philosophy Today*, XXV, 34-45.

Ekstrom, Laura Waddell. 2001. "Indeterminist Free Action." *Agency and Responsibility: Essays on the Metaphysics of Freedom*, 138-157. Ed. Laura Waddell Ekstrom. Boulder, CO, and Oxford: Westview Press.

Everson, Stephen. 1995. "[Aristotle's] Psychology." *The Cambridge Companion to Aristotle*, 168-94. Ed. Jonathan Barnes. Cambridge: Cambridge University Press.

Feinberg, Joel. 1980. "Duties, Rights, and Claims." In his *Justice, and the Bounds of Liberty:Essays in Social Philosophy*, 130-42. Princeton: Princeton University Press.

Fiering, Norman S. 1976. "Irresistible Compassion: An Aspect of Eighteenth-Century Sympathy and Humanitarianism." *Journal of the History of Ideas*, XXXVII, 2, 195-218.

Fingarette, Herbert. 1977. "Punishment as Suffering." *Proceedings and Addresses of the American Philosophical Association*, Vol. 50, no. 6: 499-525.

_____. 1979. "Following the 'One Thread' of the Analects." *The Journal of the American Academy of Religion.* Vol. 47.3, Supplementary Thematic Issue, S, 372-405.

Fletcher, Joseph. 1966. *Situation Ethics: The New Morality.* Philadelphia: Westminster Press.

Fingarette, Herbert. 1977. "Punishment as Suffering." *Proceedings and Addresses of the American Philosophical Association*, Vol. 50, no. 6: 499-525.

_____. 1979. "Following the 'One Thread' of the Analects." *The Journal of the American Academy of Religion*. Vol. 47.3, Supplementary Thematic Issue, S, 372-405.

Fletcher, Joseph. 1966. *Situation Ethics: The New Morality*. Philadelphia: Westminster Press.

Fodor, James. 2002. "Hermeneutics and the Just," in *Between the Human and the Divine: Philosophical and Theological Perspectives*, 408-26. Ed. Andrzej Wiercinski. Toronto: The Hermeneutic Press.

Forest, Jim. 1999. *The Ladder of the Beatitudes*. Maryknoll, NY: Orbis Books.

Frankfurt, Harry. 1971. "Freedom of the Will and the Concept of a Person." *The Journal of Philosophy*, LXVIII, 5-20.

Frasz, Geoffrey. 2005. "Benevolence as an Environmental Virtue." In *Environmental Virtue Ethics*, 121-34. Eds. Philip Cafaro & Ronald Sandler. Lanham, MD: Rowman & Littlefield Publishers, Inc.

Gallagher, David M. 1994. "Aquinas on Goodness and Moral Goodness." In *Thomas Aquinas and his Legacy*. David M Gallagher (Ed.). Washington, D.C.: The Catholic University of America Press.

Garfield, Jay L. 1995. "Human Rights and Compassion: Towards a Unified Moral Framework." *Journal of Buddhist Ethics* conference: http://www.buddhistethics. org/1995conf/garfield.txt

Gewirth, Alan. 1978. "The Golden Rule Rationalized." *Midwest Studies in Philosophy*, Vol. 3, 133-47.

Gould, James. 1983. "Kant's Critique of the Golden Rule." *The New Scholasticism*, Vol. 57, 115-22.

Gruzalski, Bart. 2000. *On The Buddha*. Belmont, CA: Wadsworth/Thomson Learning.

Guenther, Herbert V. 1975. "The Indivisibility of Openness and Compassion." *The Dawn of Tantra*, 26-33, by Herbert V. Guenther and Chogyam Trungpa, ed. Michael Kohn. Boulder, CO: Shambhala Publications.

Gunaratana, Henepola. 1994. *Mindfulness in Plain English*. Boston: Wisdom Publications.

Gyatso, Tenzin (see Dalai Lama)

Hanh, Thich Nhat. 1976. *Miracle of Mindfulness: An Introduction to the Practice of Meditation*. Trans. Mobi Ho. Boston: Beacon Press.

_____. 1992. *Touching Peace*. Berkeley: Parallax Press.

_____. 1999. *The Heart of the Buddha's Teaching*. New York: Broadway Books.

Hare, R.M. 1964. *The Language of Morals*. New York: Oxford University Press (Galaxy).

_____. 1965. *Freedom and Reason*. New York: Oxford University Press (Galaxy).

Harvey, Peter. 2000. *An Introduction to Buddhist Ethics: Foundations, Values and Issues*. Cambridge: Cambridge University Press.

Herman, A.L. 1979. "A solution to the paradox of desire in Buddhism." *Philosophy East and West*, 29.1, 91-94.

_____. 1980. "Ah, but there is a paradox of desire in Buddhism—A reply to Wayne Alt." *Philosophy East and West*, 30.4, 529-532.

Herzog, William R. II. 1994. *Parables as Subversive Speech: Jesus as Pedagogue of the Oppressed*, 79-97. Louisville: Westminster/John Knox Press.

Hsing Yun, Master. 1998. *Being Good: Buddhist Ethics for Everyday Life*. Trans. Tom Graham. New York & Tokyo: Weatherhill, Inc.

James, William. 1968. "The Philosopher and the Moral Life." *The Writings of William James: A Comprehensive Edition*, 610-29. Ed. John J. McDermott. New York: The Modern Library.

Jeffrey, Richard C. 1974. "Preference Among Preferences," *The Journal of Philosophy*, 71, 377-91.

Jones, Ken. 1989. *The Social Face of Buddhism: An Approach to Political and Social Activism.* Boston & London: Wisdom Publications.

Kane, Robert. 1985. *Free Will and Values.* Albany, NY: State University of New York Press.

_____. 1988. "Libertarianism and Rationality Revisited." *The Southern Journal of Philosophy*, 26, 441-60.

_____. 1996. *The Significance of Free Will.* Oxford & New York: Oxford University Press.

_____. 1999. "Responsibility, Luck and Chance: Reflections on Free Will and Indeterminism." *The Journal of Philosophy*, XCVI, 217-40.

_____. 2002. *The Oxford Handbook of Free Will.* New York: Oxford University Press.

Kant, Immanuel. 1979. *Lectures on Ethics.* Trans. L. Infield. London: Methuen Press.

_____. 1983. "Perpetual Peace." Trans. Ted Humphrey. *Perpetual Peace and Other Essays.* Indianapolis: Hackett Publishing Company.

_____. 1996a. *Groundwork of the Metaphysics of Morals.* In *Immanuel Kant: Practical Philosophy*, 41-108. Trans. and ed. by Mary J Gregor. Cambridge: Cambridge University Press.

_____. 1996b. "On a Supposed Right to Lie from Philanthropy." In *Immanuel Kant: Practical Philosophy*, 611-15. Trans. and ed. by Mary J. Gregor. Cambridge: Cambridge University Press.

_____. 1996c. *The Metaphysics of Morals.* In *Immanuel Kant: Practical Philosophy*, 353-603. Trans. and ed. by Mary J. Gregor. Cambridge: Cambridge University Press.

Keown, Damien. 1992. *The Nature of Buddhist Ethics.* New York: St. Martin's Press.

_____. 1995a. "Are there 'Human Rights' in Buddhism." *Journal of Buddhist Ethics*, 2: 3-27. http://www.buddhistethics.org/2/keown.txt

_____. 1995b. *Buddhism and Bioethics.* New York: St. Martin's Press.

King, Martin Luther Jr. 1963. "Letter from Birmingham Jail." *Why We Can't Wait*, 77-100. New York, Evanston & London: Harper & Row, 1964.

King, Winston L. 1994. "A Buddhist Ethic Without Karmic Rebirth?" *Journal of Buddhist Ethics*, Vol. 1 (online).

Kornfield, Jack. 2008. *The Wise Heart: A Guide to the Universal Teachings of Buddhist Psychology.* New York: Bantam Books.

Küng, Hans. 1976. *On Being a Christian.* Trans. Edward Quinn. Garden City: Doubleday & Company.

Laozi. 2002. *The* Daodejing *of Laozi.* Trans. Philip J. Ivanhoe. New York & London: Seven Bridges Press.

Lebacqz, Karen. 1983. "Justice, Economics, and the Uncomfortable Kingdom: Reflections on Matthew 20: 1-16." *The Annual of Society of Christian Studies*, 3, 27-53.

Levinas, Emmanuel. 1985. *Ethics and Infinity: Conversations with Philippe Nemo.* Trans. Richard A. Cohen. Pittsburgh: Duquesne University Press.

Locke, John. 1952. *The Second Treatise of Government.* Ed. Thomas P. Peardon. New York & Indianapolis: The Bobbs Merrill Company (Library of Liberal Arts).

Loori, John Daido. 1996. *The Heart of Being: Moral and Ethical Teachings of Zen Buddhism*. Eds. Bonnie Myotai Treace and Konrad Ryushin Marchaj. Boston, Rutland, VT, and Tokyo: Charles E. Tuttle Co., Inc.

MacIntyre, Alasdair. 1966. *A Short History of Ethics*. New York: The Macmillan Co.

Macy, Joanna. 1991. *World as Lover, World as Self*. Berkeley: Parallax Press.

Mannion, Gerard. 2003. *Schopenhauer, Religion and Morality: The Humble Path to Ethics*. Hants, Eng. and Burlington, VT: Ashgate Publishing Co.

Mele, Alfred (Ed.). 1997. *The Philosophy of Action*. Oxford and New York: Oxford University Press.

Merton, Thomas. 1968. *Zen and the Birds of Appetite*. New York: New Directions.

Mill, John Stuart. 1947. *On Liberty*. New York: Appleton-Century-Crofts, Inc.

_____. 1979. *Utilitarianism*. Indianapolis: Hackett Publishing Co.

Mulholland, Leslie A. 1988. "Autonomy, Extended Sympathy and the Golden Rule." *Inquiries into Values: The Inaugural Session of the Society for Value Inquiry. Problems in Contemporary Society*, Vol. 11, 89-98.

Nivison, David S. 1996. "Golden Rule Arguments in Chinese Moral Philosophy." *The Ways of Confucianism: Investigations in Chinese Philosophy*, 59-76. David S. Nivison and Bryan W. Van Norben (ed.). Chicago: Open Court Press.

Noddings, Nel. 1984. *Caring: A Feminine Approach to Ethics and Moral Education*. Berkeley & Los Angeles: Univ. of California Press.

Nussbaum, Martha. 1996. "Compassion: The Basic Social Emotion." *Social Philosophy and Policy*, 13, 27-58.

_____. 2001. *Upheavals of Thought: The Intelligence of the Emotions*. Cambridge: Cambridge University Press.

O'Connor, Timothy. 1995. *Agents, Causes, and Events: Essays on Indeterminism and Free Will*. Oxford & New York: Oxford University Press.

Passmore, John. 1975. "The Treatment of Animals." *Journal of the History of Ideas*, XXXVI, 195-218.

Patrul Rinpoche. 1998. *The Words of My Perfect Teacher*, 2nd ed. Trans. Padmakara-Translation Group. Boston: Shambhala Press.

Plato. 1945. *The Republic*. Trans. Francis Macdonald Cornford. New York and London: Oxford University Press.

_____. 1956. *Euthyphro, Apology, Crito*. Trans. F.J. Church. Indianapolis and New York: The Bobbs-Merrill Co.

_____. *Gorgias*. 1961. Trans. W.D. Woodhead. *The Collected Dialogues of Plato Including the Letters*. Eds. Edith Hamilton and Huntington Cairns. New York: Bollingen Foundation (Random House).

Pritchard, Roger. 1994. "Right Living in a Consumer Society." *Mindfulness and Meaningful Work: Explorations in Right Livelihood*: 211-13. Claude Whitmeyer (Ed). Berkeley, Parallax Press.

Radcliffe, Dana. 1994. "Compassion and Commanded Love." *Faith and Philosophy*, 11, 50-71.

Rawls, John. 1971. *A Theory of Justice*. Cambridge, MA: Harvard University Press.

Reilly, Richard. 1976. "Weakness and Blameworthiness: The Aristotelian Predicament." *Philosophical Studies* (Ireland), XXIV, 148-65.

_____. 1977a. "Moral Weakness." *International Philosophical Quarterly*, XVII, 167-77.

_____. 1977b. "Socrates' Moral Paradox." *The Southwestern Journal of Philosophy*, VIII.1, 101-7.

_____. 1979a. "Plato and Augustine on Human Weakness." *Cithara*, XVIII.2: 43-69.

_____. 1979b. "Will and the Concept of Person." *Proceedings of the American Catholic Philosophical Association*, LIII, 71-77.

_____. 2003. "Conscience, Citizenship, and Global Responsibilities." *(Journal of) Buddhist-Christian Studies*, 23, 117-31.

_____. 2006. "Compassion as Justice." *(Journal of) Buddhist-Christian Studies*, 26, 13-31.

Roberts, Robert C. 1984. "Will Power and the Virtues." *The Philosophical Review*, 97, 227-47.

Rorty, Amelie Oksenberg. 1980. "The Place of Contemplation in Aristotle's *Nicomachean Ethics.*" *Essays on Aristotle's Ethics*, 377-94. Ed. Amelie Oksenberg Rorty. Berkeley: University of California Press.

Rosen, Allen D. 1993. *Kant's Theory of Justice*. Ithaca, NY: Cornell University Press.

Ross, W.D. 1988. *The Right and the Good*. Indianapolis & Cambridge: Hackett Publishing Co.

Saddhatissa, Hammalawa. 1977. *Buddhist Ethics*, 2nd ed. Boston: Wisdom Publications.

Salzberg, Sharon. 2002. *Loving-Kindness: The Revolutionary Art of Happiness*. Boston & London: Shambhala Publications, Inc.

Santas, Gerasimos. 1964. "The Socratic Paradoxes." *The Philosophical Review*, LXXIII, 147-64.

Sartre, Jean-Paul. 1975. "Existentialism is a Humanism." Trans. Philip Mairet. *Existentialism: From Dostoevsky to Sartre* (rev. ed.). Ed. Walter Kaufmann. New York & London: New American Library (Meridian Books): 345-69.

Scheler, Max. 1954. *The Nature of Sympathy*. Trans. Peter Heath. London: Routledge & Kegan Paul.

Schopenhauer, Arthur. 1958. *The World as Will and Representation*, Vol II. Trans. E.F.G. Payne. New York: Dover Publications, Inc.

_____. 1995. *On the Basis of Morality*, rev. ed., trans. E.F.J. Payne. Providence and Oxford: Berghahan Books.

Schweitzer, Albert. 1960. *The Philosophy of Civilization*. New York: The Macmillan Company.

Shantideva. 1997. *The Way of the Bodhisattva*. Trans. Padmakara Translation Group. Boston & London: Shambhala Publications, Inc.

Singer, Marcus. 1963. "The Golden Rule." *Philosophy*, Vol. 38, 293-314.

Smith, Adam. 1969. *The Theory of Moral Sentiments*. New Rochelle, NY: Arlington House.

Smith, Huston. 1991. *The World's Religions*. New York: Harper & Row.

Snow, Nancy. 1991. "Compassion." *American Philosophical Quarterly*, 28, 195-205.

_____. 1993. "Compassion for Animals." *Between the Species: A Journal of Ethics*, 9, 61-66.

Sogyal Rinpoche. 1994. *The Tibetan Book on Living and Dying*. New York: HarperCollinsPublishers.

Spinoza, Benedict de. 1951. *The Ethics*. In *The Chief Works of Benedict de Spinoza*, II. Trans. R.H.M. Elwes. New York: Dover Publications, Inc.

Statman, Daniel. 1994. "Doing Without Mercy." *The Southern Journal of Philosophy*, XXXII, 331-54.

Stewart, Desmond. 1972. "Limits of Trooghaft." *Encounter* (Feb.)

Stump, Eleonore. 2001. "Augustine on Free Will." *The Cambridge Companion to Augustine*: 124-47. Eleonore Stump & Norman Kretzmann (Eds.). Cambridge: Cambridge University Press.

Talbott, Thomas. 1993. "Punishment, Forgiveness, and Divine Justice." *Religious Studies*, 29:151-68.

Taylor, Charles. 1999. "Sympathy." *The Journal of Ethics*, 3, 73-87.

Taylor, Richard. 1985. "Arthur Schopenhauer." *Nineteenth Century Religious Thought in the West*, Vol. 1, Ch. 5, 157-80. Eds. Ninian Smart, John Clayton, Steven Katz and Patrick Sherry. Cambridge and New York: Cambridge University Press.

———. 2000. *Good and Evil*. Amherst, NY: Prometheus Books.

Timmons, Mark. 2002. *Moral Theory: An Introduction*. Lanham, MD: Rowman & Littlefield Publishers, Inc.

Tolstoy, Leo. 2005. "Letter to Ernest Howard Crosby." *Nonviolence in Theory and Practice*, 2nd ed., 69-76. Eds. Robert L. Holmes & Barry L. Gan. Long Grove, IL: Waveland Press.

Trapp, Rainer Werner. 1998. "The Golden Rule." *Grazer philosophische Studien*, Vol. 54, 139-64.

Trungpa, Chogyam. 1993. "The Bodhisattva Path." *Entering the Stream: An Introduction to The Buddha and His Teachings*, 169-76. Eds. Samuel Bercholz and Sherab Chrodzin Kohn. Boston: Shambhala Publications, Inc.

———. 2002. *Cutting through Spiritual Materialism*. Boston: Shambhala Publications, Inc.

Ugolino di Monte Sante Maria, Bro. 1958. *The Little Flowers of St. Francis*. Trans. Raphael Brown. Garden City, NY: Doubleday & Company (Image Books).

Visader, John. 1978. "The use of paradox in uroboric philosophies." *Philosophy East and West* 28.4, 455-67.

———. 1980. "A reply to Wayne Alt's 'There is no paradox of desire in Buddhism.'" *Philosophy East and West*, 30.4, 533-34.

Wallace, B. Alan. 1999. *Boundless Heart: The Cultivation of the Four Immeasurables*. Ithaca, NY: Snow Lion Publications.

Wang, Quingjie James. 1999. "The Golden Rule and Interpersonal Care—From a Confucian Perspective." *Philosophy East & West*. Vol. 49.4, 415-38.

Wattles, Jeffrey. 1987. "Levels of Meaning in the Golden Rule." *The Journal of Religious Ethics*, Vol. 15.1, 106-29.

———. 1996. *The Golden Rule*. New York & Oxford: Oxford University Press.

Weil, Simone. 1977. "Human Personality" [aka, "Beyond Personalism"], *The Simone Weil Reader*, 313-39. Ed. George A. Panichas. New York: David McKay Company, Inc.

Weile, Jos V.M. 1995. "Sympathy as the Basis of Compassion." *Cambridge Quarterly of Healthcare Ethics*, 4, 476-87.

Wilkes, Kathleen V. 1980. "The Good Man and the Good for Man in Aristotle's Ethics." *Essays on Aristotle's Ethics*, 341-57. Ed. Amelie Oksenberg Rorty. Berkeley: University of California Press.

Wilson, Jack. 1999. *Biological Individuality: The Identity and Persistence of Living Entities*. Cambridge: Cambridge University Press.

Wolf, Susan. 1990. *Freedom Within Reason*. New York and Oxford: Oxford University Press.

Wood, Allen W. 2008. *Kantian Ethics*. Cambridge: Cambridge University Press.

Wilkes, Kathleen V. 1980. "The Good Man and the Good for Man in Aristotle's Ethics." *Essays on Aristotle's Ethics*, 341-57. Ed. Amelie Oksenberg Rorty. Berkeley: University of California Press.

Wilson, Jack. 1999. *Biological Individuality: The Identity and Persistence of Living Entities*. Cambridge: Cambridge University Press.

Wolf, Susan. 1990. *Freedom Within Reason*. New York and Oxford: Oxford University Press.

Wood, Allen W. 2008. *Kantian Ethics*. Cambridge: Cambridge University Press.

Index

Mill, John Stuart, 54, 69, 95
Mindfulness, 80-83, 87
Montaigne, Michel de, 37
Morality,
    moral choice, 70-71, 102-3, 105,
    110-11, 114-16
    moral nature, 47, 50
    moral obligation, 40-41, 44, 48, 58,
    71, 84
    moral rules, 57, 67-71 (see
    Precepts)
    moral theory, 2-5
    moral value, 49-50, 56, 69-71, 113-
    14
    moral weakness, see Will,
    weakness of
    and state, 84-86
Moral paradox, 75
Mulholland, Leslie A., 14-15

Naess, Arne, 86
Nagel, Thomas, 30
Nash, Arthur, 16-17
Natural Law, 58, 67
Need(s), 45, 48, 52, 62-63, 70, 90
Nietzsche, Friedrich, 23, 25, 35
Nivison, David S, 11, 18
Noddings, Nel, 41, 48, 68-69
Nussbaum, Martha, 3, 22-24, 35-36, 37,
    76

O'Connor, Timothy, 121
Oliner, Sam (and Pearl), 21-23, 27, 28,
    33, 35, 45, 46, 49, 71

Pain, 29-32, 44 (see Suffering)
Paramitas, 2, 4, 74, 77-80, 90
Participation (emotional) 22, 27-34, 36,
    55
Passmore, John, 37
Paul, St., 95, 124
Patience, 4, 78-80, 82, 86, 118
Patrul Rinpoche, 54
Peace, 85-86
Pelagian controversy, 121
Penney, J.C., 16
Peter the Great, 123
Piety, 19
Pity, 1, 3, 21-26, 31, 35-36, 44, 55
Plato, 1, 7, 45, 54, 74-76, 94, 102, 119,
    122

Poeman, Abbot, 119
Praise(worthy), 78, 98-99, 116-17, 120
Precepts, 2, 4, 7, 41, 46, 53, 57-73, 80-84,
    87, 118
Preferences, 102-104, 108-116
Practical syllogism (reasoning), 99, 120-
    21
Principles (moral), 4, 39, 41-45, 47, 59-
    50, 73, 80, 99
Pritchard, Roger, 83
Prudential choice, 70, 105-8, 111, 114
Prudential paradox, 75
Punishment, 98, 100, 116, 119-20, 122
Purity (of heart), 50, 123-25

Radcliffe, Dana, 40, 50, 53
Rawls, John, 46
Reason(s) for acting/choosing, 106-116,
    124
Real Self View, 5, 112-16
Reason View, 5, 112-16
Reilly, Richard, 72, 94, 95, 101, 121
Renunciation, 90
Responsibility, 45, 82, 97-102, 111-21
Responsiveness, 26, 28, 33-34, 90, 125
Retribution, 19, 61, 85
Revenge, see Vengence
Right Conduct, 58-67
Righteous gentiles, 3, 21, 35
Rights (human), 2, 84-85
Roberts, Robert C., 40
Romanticism, 23
Rosen, Allen D., 55
Rorty, Amelie O., 94
Ross, W.D., 45
Rousseau, Jean Jacques, 22, 84
Rules, 67-71 (see Precepts)

Saddhatissa, Hammalawa, 59, 77-78, 82
Salzberg, Sharon, 125
Santas, Gerasimos, 94
Sartre, Jean-Paul, 5, 97-98, 102-4, 113,
    116, 121
Satan, 101
Sauvage, Pierre, 36
Scheler, Max, 29-30, 34-37
Schopenhauer, Arthur, 1-3, 22-23, 25,
    27-29, 34, 35, 41-42, 44, 46, 54, 63, 70
Schweitzer, Albert, 39, 43, 50, 53, 82
Self-centeredness, 60, 62-63, 73-74, 78,